More Praise for *Teach Anyone To Read: The No-Nonsense Guide*

"It is not often that an educator comes across a work that ignores the language of the reading wars and provides a practical, easy to use and comprehensive guide to teaching reading. Students who have taken my literacy courses and are now teaching, have commented on the enormous value of having been introduced to literacy instruction through Dr. Pope's principles, from assessment through to remediation. In fact, the book provides detailed follow-up practices that can be used to address the problems uncovered through evaluation. This aspect of the book is critical to literacy training because student teachers are often taught to diagnose reading problems but not given methods to remediate the areas of weakness. I recommend this resource to instructors who want to provide their students with a clear understanding of reading problems and practical methods with which to address them."

—*Marie C. White, Assist. Prof., Deputy Chair,*
Childhood and Early Childhood Education
Nyack College School of Education

In Kazakhstan, students who suffer from difficulties or disabilities in learning language are expected to learn in the same environment with students who learn at a normal pace. Using the methods in this book, I have been able to introduce, not only to my students, but also to local teachers, new ways to give these students an opportunity to approach the English language at their own pace.

—*Sam Robinson, Peace Corps volunteer, Kazakhstan*

Practical, direct, thorough and eminently readable, *Teach Anyone To Read: The No-Nonsense Guide* is truly a no-nonsense guide to teaching reading, and much, much more. This book looks as carefully at the situation in which one teaches and one learns, as it does at the techniques for teaching. It builds the necessary understanding of the social context in a clear and precise manner, just as it presents the actual steps to teaching reading. For the teacher, specialist, allied professional, parent, volunteer and all who are committed to taking on the challenge of improving literacy in our country this is an important work.

—*Deborah Edel, Head, Division of Psychological*
Support Services, Director of Admissions,
Mary McDowell Center for Learning

See back cover for additional comments.

Teach Anyone To Read: The No-Nonsense Guide

For the:

- **Novice**—Parent Volunteers, Lay Persons

- **Paraprofessional**—Education Assistants

- **Professional**—Teachers K-12, Adult Basic Education Programs, Guidance Counselors and Auxiliary Professionals

- **Homeschooler**

- **Teacher Trainers**—in College Graduate Pre-Teaching Programs

- **Teachers of English as a Second Language**

Lillie Pope, Ph.D

EJK Press
New York

Revised and Updated from the original work
Guidelines for Teaching Reading Copyright © 1996

Teach Anyone To Read: The No-Nonsense Guide
ISBN: 978-1-60402-148-6

Published by EJK Press
Ezra Jack Keats Foundation
450 14th Street
Brooklyn, New York 11215

Book design and alphabet illustrations: Jeanette Levy
Dragon illustrations: Karli Tucker
Cover photo: Liz Sullivan
Art Direction: Deborah Pope

Manufactured in the United States

To the winter soldiers, those who teach and those who learn.

Acknowledgments

I have been inspired and encouraged to revise this book for the twenty-first century by the many readers of my previous work, and attendees of my workshops and lectures. They have reported that my book has helped make their work more successful. I trust that this will continue to be true.

In addition, I am grateful to Dr. Sasha Durandin for technical assistance, to Dr. Abraham George for advice, and to Ethel Tucker for encouragement and reviewing the manuscript in its present form. Dr. Deborah Pope has made an enormous contribution by transforming the book into the style of the twenty-first century. I am deeply grateful to her; to my husband, Dr. Martin Pope, who has taken time from his independent studies to assist me in every way possible; and to Miriam Pope, whose gifted teaching of children with special needs has long been an inspiration to me.

I must add a "thank you" to the internet, which has invidiously entered the field of communications and replaced the typewriter, carbon paper and the eraser, forgiving a multitude of errors, and providing names, addresses and telephone numbers when needed.

Other books by Lillie Pope include:

Word Play, A Dictionary of Idioms

Tutor

Guidelines to Teaching Children with Learning Problems

Co-author:

Special Needs, Special Answers

Psycho-Educational Evaluation of the Pre-School Child

Table of Contents

Table of Contents

Table of Contents

Part V: Support Materials

Table of Contents

Preface

It is shocking to realize that illiteracy is still expanding despite ever more sophisticated teaching methods, heightened awareness of the importance of literacy and the spread of computers and internet use. The population of non-readers includes both children who, for a variety reasons, fail to learn the necessary skills in the classroom and adults who cannot decipher instructions, contracts, warnings on medications or simple books their children bring home from school.

The good news is that breaking the barrier to literacy is an achievable goal. The difference between failure and success lies in effective teaching. My aim in this book is to show how, with proper instruction, educators and students can meet that goal.

This book covers specific techniques for teaching children, adolescents and adults to read, explaining sophisticated methods simply and without jargon. It discusses the relationship between the instructor and the student, outlines in simple terms the skills involved in the act of reading and shows how to evaluate the student's reading level and determine his or her strengths and weaknesses. Finally, it offers guidance in organizing an effective program of instruction, helpful tips and suggestions of materials that will be useful in reading programs with limited funds. In short, this is a no-nonsense, hands-on book, based on solid educational success.

This book has been used successfully by thousands of instructors, from novices to experienced professionals. They include teachers and other school personnel, people in the helping professions, peer-tutors and dedicated volunteers who fit none of the above categories. Not only have they been able to help many thousands of students learn to read, but many report that they themselves have gained much from the process. It is never too late to learn!

A Note on Gender

Many more boys than girls have difficulty learning to read. Although many attempts have been made to understand this discrepancy, we have no proven, scientific explanation. Some researchers suggest that the causes are mainly cultural, while others point to biological factors. Whatever the reason, instructors working with reluctant readers in elementary, intermediate and high schools will be teaching more boys than girls.

In contrast, there are more women than men in adult programs and in classes where English is taught as a second language. It is possible that this imbalance is a reflection of men's greater discomfort with admitting to having a problem learning to read. It may also be due to the fact that men who are unable to read often work in jobs involving heavy or menial labor, causing them to be too exhausted to attend an evening class.

In order to be fair to both sexes, this book uses the male and female pronouns in an essentially random fashion, leaving it up to the reader to choose the appropriate pronoun.

Introduction

Reading instruction in the last fifty years has been polarized between the traditional Phonics approach (also known as the Decoding, or Teaching of Skills, approach) and the more recent Whole Language approach (also called the Sight Word, or Balanced Reading, approach). In a sense, this is good, because it is a measure of the passion invested by instructors in their work. Both methods strive to cultivate pride and joy in learning, and both require teaching environments in which:

- the learner is encouraged, through the presence of many varied books and activities, to explore and learn.

- all the language arts—reading, writing, listening and speaking—are emphasized and integrated.

- the learner has access to many books and is guided to write a lot.

- the learner is encouraged to speak as well as listen.

These approaches are not mutually exclusive, and in the hands of an enthusiastic, knowledgeable, hard-working instructor, either one can be successful.

In the Phonics, or Teaching of Skills, approach, the reader learns the sounds represented by individual letters and then sounds out the words. In the Whole Language, or Sight Word, approach, the beginner is taught to recognize whole words by their shape and appearance. The underlying premise of the Whole Language approach is that learning to read is a spontaneous skill. This works well for some beginners—and for some advanced readers as well. Many students, however, do not learn to read spontaneously.

Instruction in specific skills is helpful to all learners. It has been found that a greater number of students succeed in learning to read when they are taught with the sounding-out approach. Additionally, all students learn more easily with a multi-sensory approach, which is described on page 21.

However, there are some commonly used sight words that should be taught early in order to help the student read sentences more quickly and understand what he is reading. These are articles and connecting words, like *and* and *the*, which are the building blocks of sentences. In this way, the reading instruction can be made meaningful and relevant to the learner's interests and needs.

In my experience, success in teaching depends to a large degree on the quality of the teachers and the climate for learning in the classroom. The most successful teachers are those who are open-minded, flexible and prepared to adapt their teaching to the individual needs of their students.

This book does not dictate that any one program is suitable for all learners, but it does provide suggestions to help teachers plan for each individual. Many instructions are repeated often. This repetition is intended. It is an example of what the instructor must do in order to succeed with the student.

Go forth and tame dragons!

How to Use this Book

Before You Meet Your Students

1. Read Part I carefully.

2. Skim through Parts II and III to acquaint yourself with the type of information provided.

After You Meet Your Students

1. Get to know your students and their interests.

2. Determine the students' reading levels. See pages 99–208.

   a. If at the third grade level or below, see pages 125–145.

   b. If at the fourth grade level or above, see pages 147–157.

3. Determine your students' reading requirements and plan your instruction.

   a. If at the third grade level or below:
      Teaching of Target skills, see pages 125–145.
      Suggestions for correcting bad reading habits, pages 225–229.
      Applicable word lists, see pages 172–218.
      Useful games, see pages 161–170.

   b. If at the fourth to eighth grade reading level:
      Teaching of Target skills, see pages 148–149.
      Suggestions for correcting bad reading habits, pages 225–229.
      Applicable word lists, see pages 172–218.
      Useful games, see pages 161–170.

   c. If at the ninth grade level and above:
      Teaching of Target skills, see pages 151–155.
      Suggestions for correcting bad reading habits, pages 225–229.
      Word lists, see pages 172–218.
      GED High School Equivalency Exam, pages 156–157.

NOPQRSTUV
WXYZABCDE
FGHIJKLMN
OPQRSTUVW
XYZABCDEF
GHIJKLMNO
PQRSTUVWX
YZABCDEFG
HIJKLMNOPQ
RSTUVWXYZ

Part I
Background

Teach Anyone To Read: The No-Nonsense Guide

Chapter 1: Before You Begin

Why Is Reading Difficult?

This poem makes the point all too well:

Hints on Pronunciation

I take it you already know
Of tough and bough and cough and dough?
Others may stumble but not you
On Hiccough, thorough, laugh and through.
Well done! And now you wish, perhaps,
To learn of less familiar traps?
Beware of heard, a dreadful word
That looks like beard, and sounds like bird,
And dead: it's said like bed, not bead—
For goodness' sake don't call it "deed"!
Watch out for meat and great and threat
(They rhyme with suite and straight and debt.)
A moth is not a moth in mother
Nor both in bother, broth in brother,
And here is not a match for there
Nor dear and fear for bear and pear.
And then there's dose and rose and lose—
Just look them up—and goose and choose.
And cork and work and card and ward,
And font and front and word and sword,
And do and go and thwart and cart--
Come, come, I've hardly made a start!
A dreadful language? Man alive.
I'd mastered it when I was five.

From a letter published in the *London Sunday Times* (January 3, 1965), cited by Chomsky (1970) and by Adams, *Beginning to Read* (1990)

Why Students Want to Learn to Read

All students have very specific goals, ranging from the most modest to the most challenging. These are some common goals:

- to be able to keep up in school.

- to be able to read street and subway signs.

- to increase self-respect and respect from others.

- to be able as an immigrant to function more comfortably in this country.

- to be able to read documents requiring a signature, such as leases and contracts.

- to be able to fill out an application for a job.

- to be able to read a book.

- to be able to read the Bible.

- to be able to help their children with school work.

- to learn to be better parents.

- to have a social outlet—to have something to do and someone to talk to.

- to be able to read newspapers and magazines.

- to be able to read on a higher level in order to qualify for a better job.

- to be able to acquire a High School Equivalency Certificate (GED)—a minimum requirement for many jobs that offer opportunities to advance, and for the possibility of higher education.

- as a tool for getting information and learning

- for pleasure.

What Is Reading?

The most important and basic tool for learning is reading. Most of us have never thought about what is involved in the effort of reading. When we speak of reading we refer to a complex act, consisting of two major processes. The first process involves perceiving the printed symbol (a letter or a word) and associating with it the sound or sounds that it represents. For example, in reading the word *goat*, the reader says three basic sounds, represented by *g*, *o* and *t*, combining them to say the whole word. Sounding out the printed letters is called decoding the symbol. The second process involves understanding the meaning of the symbols. Thus, a goat is understood to be a particular kind of animal.

Both processes are essential for reading. Reading without understanding is useless, and understanding is impossible without decoding the printed symbol. Reading instruction, therefore, must focus on teaching the student how to decode the printed symbol and helping him understand what he reads.

How Many Students Are Failing To Learn?

According to some estimates, one in every five schoolchildren has difficulty learning; others put the figure at only one in twenty. Experts tell us that in every supposedly normal classroom in the nation, there are quite a few students whose difficulty in learning is unidentified and who need special assistance to prevent them from failing. No matter which numbers are correct, it is undeniably true that in this country, it is

judged that approximately 20 percent of adults cannot pass a fourth-grade elementary school reading test.

You must keep these goals in mind, the better to motivate your students to learn and sustain their interest. Try at all times to make reading pleasurable so that your students will widen their horizons and deepen their enjoyment of life. As they succeed, their self-image will improve and their confidence in their ability to learn will grow.

Learning to read English is difficult because the way words are spelled doesn't always indicate how they sound. For example, *read* can sound like *reed* or like *red*, and of course, each spelling or pronunciation has a different meaning. The beginning reader learns that certain sounds are associated with certain symbols. Usually, when he sees *s*, he should say *ss*, but sometimes the s sounds like *zz*; thus, in the word *sings*, each s has a different sound. When followed by *h*, as in *sh*, it has another, completely different sound. *K* is usually pronounced *kuh*; but sometimes it has no sound at all, as in *know*. Furthermore, the same sound may be written in unrelated ways. For example, the *zh* sound is the same in the words *azure*, *pleasure* and *rouge*, yet the spelling is completely different.

A major difficulty in learning to read involves recognizing the letters. A small child learns that a chair is a chair, no matter which way it faces, whether it is upside down on a table or standing upright on the floor. When the child sees the letters *p*, *b*, *d* and *q*, they all look like the same letter except that each one faces in a different direction. The student must learn that letters are not like other objects. Those remain the same whatever their orientation, while letters change depending on which way they are turned. The concept that things can look the same yet be quite different can be confusing. As a further complication, the beginning reader must learn that some letters look different but mean the same thing, such as capital and small letters like *a* and *A*.

The student must also know the difference between left and right—and must learn that in English, readers begin at the left and read systematically across the page to the right end of the line—and then jump back to the left of the very next line to repeat the process.

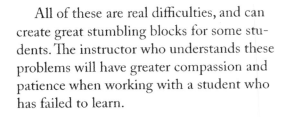

This one drug dealer said to me, 'the scariest thing to a kid out here on the street is not drugs, AIDS, guns, jail, death. It's words on a page. Because if a 15-year-old kid could handle words on a page, he'd be home doing his homework instead of selling dope with me.'

The New York Times
11/6/92

All of these are real difficulties, and can create great stumbling blocks for some students. The instructor who understands these problems will have greater compassion and patience when working with a student who has failed to learn.

Why Some People Have Difficulty Learning to Read

Learning difficulties can be caused by a number of factors, including physical and emotional problems, poor environment and ineffective teaching.

- **Physical Problems**

Since reading depends so heavily on the senses of seeing and hearing, any student with a problem in either area will have special difficulty. If you think that your student has a problem with his vision or hearing, make sure he is evaluated quickly so that the problem can be corrected.

Some students have subtle neurological problems that make it more difficult for them to learn to read: they have difficulty expressing themselves, processing language or making some of the associations that are necessary in reading. They may have been diagnosed with dyslexia, attention deficit disorder or another learning disability, and would certainly benefit from supplementary assistance.

You may encounter a student who is not learning because of limited intellectual capacity (sometimes referred to as low IQ). However, the number of such people in the general population is small, and chances are that few, if any, of your students have this problem.

Your basic assumption must be that each student can learn more than he has in the past and that you can help him do so.

• Environmental Problems

From birth, every individual is exposed to the many different sounds and sights of home and neighborhood. But the child who has been drawn into few conversations or discussions will lack the vocabulary to express feelings or describe many things and ideas. If, for example, no one has ever chatted with a child about big and small, tomorrow and yesterday, the days of the week or the months of the year, these concepts will be vague for him. If no one reads to him, shows him pictures or describes new sights outside his little world, or if there are no pencils or paper in the home, he will be handicapped as a reader even when he becomes an adolescent or an adult.

You are in a position to help compensate for this early lack of stimulation and experience. Whether your student is a child or an adult, conversation and reading aloud can help overcome this early handicap.

Students who come from a home where a foreign language is spoken may have the necessary vocabulary and concepts—but only in their mother tongue. Their difficulty may simply be a lack of familiarity with the sounds of the English language. Conversation in English is particularly important for them.

Children who come from homes in which education is not highly valued are often not expected to succeed at school. This may be the attitude of their parents, and in some cases, their teachers as well. Unfortunately, such children can easily absorb the feeling that learning is not really worth the trouble it takes.

It should be remembered that people generally rise to meet expectations: if you expect your student to work hard and succeed, your attitude will have a positive effect on his attitude toward learning.

• Emotional Problems

Reading difficulties are inevitably intertwined with emotional problems. Even when emotional problems are not the primary cause, they are bound to develop with every failure. The student who fails can easily come to believe that she is stupid, inadequate and worthless. Her behavior reflects these feelings and serves as a further deterrent to learning, causing her to withdraw from the learning situation. Unable to pay attention, she becomes impatient, which may be translated into restlessness. She may seek another outlet for her energies and become disruptive in class.

Some children, when they feel stupid, try to make themselves invisible in the classroom. They hope that the teacher will not call on them, so that their ignorance will not be exposed repeatedly. They sit quietly daydreaming, often unnoticed by the teacher because they do not interfere with the work of the class. Their learning failures are thereby compounded by lack of attention.

Problem readers are all too often seen as "bad" children, and they see themselves as "bad" children. They can be impatient and restless or withdrawn and unresponsive. While they may appear competent or insist with bravado that they know it all or that they just don't care, such children, in fact, suffer from a lack of self-esteem. Convinced that they are hopeless failures, they lose all confidence that they can learn. As they grow older, the lack of basic reading skills dooms them to continued failure in school. As their feelings of unhappiness pile up, many of these students are increasingly absent from school, until they give up and drop out altogether.

- **Inadequate Schooling**

Inadequate, insufficient and inappropriate teaching accounts for some students' failure to learn to read. A specific teaching method may be appropriate for many students in the class, and they will make good progress. However, the same teaching method is probably inappropriate for the few students who are not learning. Their learning needs may require a different approach. As illustrated in the poem "Hints on Pronunciation" on page 10, the English language has a number of quirks that make it difficult for some to learn to read.

Your class may be the first opportunity that some students have had to go to school! But once you convince them that it is not too late to start, even this group can learn quickly.

Additional Causes for Learning Difficulties

- They are hungry when they come to school, and therefore have difficulty paying attention.

- They are "late bloomers," who need a little more time to develop some of the basic learning skills.

- They are very active children, who have not learned to concentrate for long enough on classroom activities.

- The teacher does not expect them to learn.

Since causes are rarely simple or isolated, it is probable that a combination of factors has contributed to a student's failure. This book concentrates on the general requirements for the teaching of reading and can therefore be used to assist an instructor in dealing with these complex issues in any type of reading program.

However, it is important to remember that there is no magic formula; you can help a student open the door to learning, but the student must walk through. You need to convey your confidence in your student and your belief that learning to read will enable him to lead a fuller, more rewarding life as time goes on.

The purpose of this book is to help you do your job. Review it carefully after you have met your students, paying special attention to the sections that deal specifically with students like yours and marking sections for later reference.

Teaching is a rewarding experience. Be patient. As your students learn, you will, too.

Teach Anyone To Read: The No-Nonsense Guide

Chapter 2: After You Meet Your Student

What Behaviors Do We See?

Adolescents and adults who have failed to learn usually could have been identified as needing assistance when they were children. Here are some of the behaviors you may encounter as you sit down to work with your student:

- He always needs a drink of water.

- He needs to leave the room just after the whole class has returned from an outing.

- He is fascinated by a fly buzzing near a neighbor's desk.

- He is caught up in daydreams and misses most of what goes on at the front of the classroom.

- He pokes the boy nearby because things are getting a bit dull where he is.

- He keeps losing his place.

- He can never find his homework, a pencil or a tissue.

- He is always dropping things, spilling milk or bumping into things.

- He reads words backwards and skips lines or words.

- When he tries to write, the letters are uneven, backwards or hard to recognize.

- She always pays attention to the wrong things.

- She does not know left from right.

- She acts without thinking or does the same thing again and again, even when it is no longer appropriate.

- She is good in the morning and irritable in the afternoon.

- She knows something perfectly one day and does not know it at all the next day.

- She is slow to finish the work

- She interprets everything you say quite literally. When she hears an expression like "It's so confusing, it makes my head spin," she looks to see whether your head is really spinning.

The net effect of these behaviors is that the student feels frustrated and inadequate. Somehow the others seem to have learned something that she did not. She feels stupid.

What Do These Students Need?

On the simplest and most compelling level, children, adolescents and adults who have failed to learn need to know someone who listens to them, trusts them, has confidence in them and treats them with courtesy, respect and appreciation. They need to know someone who understands that a thirst for knowledge, the ability to work in order to learn and, in many cases, the ability to control oneself are more immediately important than getting regular haircuts or dressing in a suit and tie. They need an instructor who has the time to focus on them. They need encouragement to develop skills and inspiration to use them.

Can You Really Help?

Because the classroom teacher is responsible for the whole class, he may frequently find it difficult, if not impossible, to give each child individual attention. For example, the teacher of a fifth-grade class may give a lagging student a third-grade reader, thinking that it will take care of the problem. However, this may embarrass the child, who may be lost at that reading level as well. The secret of success in this case is to have a reading instructor work with the student one-on-one or in a small group to find out precisely what skills the student needs to learn and to teach her at the appropriate level.

To build a positive relationship with the student, the instructor needs to be respectful, kind, consistent and honest. His time and his undivided attention whenever possible, are precious gifts to the student. By offering solid support in the areas in which the student lacks skills, the instructor can build a firm foundation for the student's continued success.

Rather than saying that he will "teach the student to read," it is preferable for the instructor to say that he will "try to help her learn." In this way the student can take full credit for her accomplishments.

NOTES

Teach Anyone To Read: The No-Nonsense Guide

Chapter 3: What to Know About Good Teaching

Principles of Teaching and Learning

The following principles are important in teaching students of all ages, individually or in groups. They are essential in dealing with students requiring individualized instruction, who have failed to learn to read in the past and will not succeed now without special attention.

- **Remember that each individual is different.**

You can best help each student by comparing his progress with his previous work, not that of his brothers, sisters, parents or classmates.

- **Learn by doing: the Multi-sensory Approach.**

We learn by means of information sent to our brains by our senses—seeing, hearing, touching, tasting and smelling—and moving our muscles. If any of the senses is impaired, or if the brain cannot interpret the information transmitted, we will have difficulty learning. Those problems can usually be overcome with careful, attentive instruction.

In the traditional classroom, children sit at their desks most of the day and listen to the teacher. They are exposed mainly to oral instruction, and are expected to learn primarily by listening and secondarily by looking. But nowadays, many classrooms are set up with activity centers. As the children go from one activity to another, they look, listen, touch, taste, smell and move. They learn by doing—the most effective way to acquire any skill.

The flexible teacher has the great advantage of permitting the student to learn through all of his senses, using a "multi-sensory approach." Imagine learning how to drive a car, or how to swim, by listening to a lecture that describes all of the movements to be learned. Only by "doing" can these skills be learned properly. The same holds true for reading.

Not only is it easier for individuals to learn when information comes in through all of the senses, it is also more enjoyable. Restless students can move around and use materials that are colorful and interesting. Students who have had difficulty keeping up in a large classroom will find that learning by doing provides more pleasure, success and satisfaction.

> *An old Chinese proverb:*
> *I hear, and I forget,*
> *I see, and I remember,*
> *I do, and I understand.*

The multi-sensory approach can be tailored to the individual's needs and interests. It recognizes and respects the fact that each student is unique and merits a personalized approach.

- **Keep the student interested at all times.**

If the student is not interested, he will not learn. Although he may be reluctant to read, the time you spend together should be centered on some area in which he takes a special interest. This may be baking or cooking for one child, and dinosaurs for another. A recent immigrant may be most interested in how to cope with the demands of daily life, such as shopping or dealing with social agencies.

Reading skills can then be related to these particular areas of interest.

Each student can:

- talk about the subject.
- do research on the subject with the instructor.
- become involved in activities related to the subject.
- dictate stories about it.
- write about it.

In this way, the student learns reading skills at his own level while relating to his area of interest, and at the same time learns how to find out things for herself.

If the student has difficulty in understanding information that comes to him via one sensory channel, he may receive and understand more efficiently through the other senses. Remember that a child can learn a lot through the muscles, and moving around helps release pent-up energy. If he is learning the letter *t*, for example, you can have him:

- write it in the air.

- shape it with his body.

- shape it out of clay.

- feel it on sandpaper.

- trace it on acetate.

- trace it in sand.

- write it on the chalkboard (this uses the large muscles).

- write it on paper (this uses the small muscles).

- shape it out of licorice, and then eat it.

- feel a t-shaped alphabet cracker with his finger and eat it.

- say a word beginning with the *t* sound as he performs each of these tasks.

Although such tasks may sound simple, some learners find them difficult at first.

Teach Anyone To Read: The No-Nonsense Guide

- **Make reading pleasurable for the students.**

Spend some time every day reading to your students: select a joke, a short story, a recipe or some book that interests them. This helps associate a feeling of pleasure with the printed word.

Not only are games fun to play, they are also helpful in teaching reading skills. Many teachers and tutors are reluctant to play reading games because the activity takes so much time; they are impatient for students to learn despite past failures. Enjoyable tasks related to reading skills do help students learn more quickly.

- **Choose your words carefully.**

In the traditional classroom, the teacher talks much of the time, and students are required to listen. Many students have difficulty paying attention to the constant stream of "teacher talk" and stop listening. This is a powerful lesson. Be careful not to talk too much, or your student will tune you out, too. Make sure that you encourage the student to talk, as well as do, during the session.

If your student is learning English as a second language, be certain that he understands the words that you use. Some individuals tend to be very literal in their thinking. Thus, if they hear someone say, "I was crushed when I heard the news," they could be confused by the use of the word *crushed* as a description of an emotional response. If your student tends to think in this fashion, try to avoid using idioms, phrases and words that may disconcert him. Explain the meaning of each expression that is confusing, and help him use it in a sentence.

It is necessary to speak simply, clearly and respectfully. At the same time, be careful not to talk down to the student.

- **Encourage oral expression.**

Improvement in oral expression is an important goal for a student who is learning to read. With increased practice, she will improve her vocabulary, formulate thoughts in an orderly way and thus learn to communicate more effectively. When you converse with your student, frame your own sentences to encourage a thoughtful response. Avoid questions that can be answered "yes" or "no," as this allows a discouraged learner to remain silent. Instead of asking, "Did you like the show on TV last night?" try, "What did you think of the show?" or "Tell me what the show was about."

If you are teaching in your student's neighborhood, walk around and become familiar with it. This will help you know your student better and give you something more to talk about with her.

- **Plan many activities within the reading period.**

Hold the student's attention by preparing many activities for each lesson. For a lesson lasting forty minutes, be prepared with at least eight activities. These activities may be designed to teach the same skill approached from several different angles, or they may have different goals. For example, each activity used in teaching the letter *b*, listed on page 130, lasts just long enough to hold the student's attention. Most students who have failed are restless, so it is helpful to plan activities that give the student an opportunity to move around between sedentary tasks. Learn how long your student can stay on task, and then shift to a new activity before she wearies of the previous one.

Remember that one of the activities in each lesson should be your reading something of great interest to the student; a conversation about her special concerns is important in encouraging her to express herself and helpful in building her self-esteem.

- **Plan each lesson, and keep notes.**

Your notes and your lesson plans will remind you of what your students knew when you began and ended each session, and will help you plan clearly for the next lesson. They will also make it easier for your supervisor to help guide you, and for a substitute teacher to step in when you are sick or called away. Your notes will also remind you of important details, such as a student's nickname and birthday or problems that he has mentioned that should be shared with your supervisor.

It is your responsibility both to plan carefully for the lesson and to be flexible, taking your cues from your student. Build on the student's strengths and interests. Remember, the girl who likes to cook will learn to read recipes even though she may resist formal reading instruction.

It is important to plan for the student to make some progress each day and to be aware of her success. Without planning, the possibility of failure and frustration rises significantly. This could be disastrous for someone who has not succeeded in the past. Your student should leave each lesson with a real sense of enjoyment and achievement.

Keep an accurate attendance record. It will help you later in evaluating progress.

- **Use tactile, colorful materials.**

Use materials that can be handled and manipulated whenever possible. Different textures and attractive colors are stimulating to the senses and the imagination, and will make each activity more memorable. Use your own imagination and whatever you have around you to produce materials that you and your student can use to shape and trace letters, words and numbers, and to mount her written material and make books that she will write and illustrate.

These are some materials that can be used imaginatively; I'm sure that you can list at least ten more on this page.

• crayon	• pipe cleaners	_____
• paint	• licorice strips	_____
• acetate	• magazine pictures	_____
• felt	• construction paper	_____
• velvet	• tissue paper	_____
• sand	• crepe paper	_____
• Magic Markers	• wool	_____
• felt-tip pens	• cloth of different	_____
• sandpaper	colors and textures	_____
• cookies		_____

- **Be clear about the rules.**

  Your student will welcome knowing what to
  expect and what she is allowed to do and not
  to do. In other words, let her know "the rules of
  the game," and stick to them. Some things are
  never allowed: the student is never permitted
  to hurt another person, act in a dangerous or
  threatening manner or destroy equipment.
  Some rules may be imposed by you, and some
  by the school. Typically, it is not permitted:

  - to run and shout in the corridor.

  - to take a drink of water more
    often than specified.

  - to go to the bathroom more
    often than specified.

  - to be late to a session.

  - to miss a session without notice.

  - to interrupt another student's session.

  - to leave a session early,
    without prior planning.

  - to disturb others who are working.

  The rules should be clear, and you must
  be consistent about adhering to them. The
  student is more secure when she knows how
  her world operates.

- **Don't promise what you can't deliver.**

To have confidence in you, your student must know that you always keep your word. Therefore, be cautious; promise only what you know you can deliver. It is poor practice to promise something that depends on another person, who may fail to deliver to you, causing you, in turn, to disappoint your student. Thus, if you plan to lend a book that you like, promise it only if you yourself have it at home and can bring it in. If you plan to borrow the book from the library, it may not be available when you go to pick it up. As a result, you will have failed to keep your word.

- **Focus on your goal, and do not criticize irrelevancies.**

Your primary goal is to help the student learn how to read. You will discover that he has many problems in addition to those related to reading. He may come in unprepared. His speech may be ungrammatical and his vocabulary earthy. His fingernails and clothes may be dirty. Do not criticize any of this— concentrate only on reading. If he is a young child and you inquire about his cleanliness, he will interpret it as a reflection on his family and his background, and his self-esteem will be further injured. Accept him as he is. Respect him for his positive qualities and focus on the subject matter at hand.

If you find that the student has other problems that are urgent, discuss them with the appropriate person, who should then attend to them promptly. In this way, disruptive personal problems will be taken care of, while your relationship with the student remains uncomplicated.

- **Keep your schedule of reading lessons regular and evenly spaced.**

Psychologists tell us that we learn more quickly when our lessons are evenly spaced throughout the week rather than concentrated in one day. Investing the same amount of time in several shorter sessions, the student will be less fatigued at the end of each session and will have less time between sessions to forget what was learned. Although daily reading instruction is not practical for many people, schedule as many sessions as possible per week. Learning will be very slow and frustrating if the student has fewer than two sessions each week.

- **Provide for much repetition and practice.**

Memory and learning are closely related. The student with learning problems often forgets easily and needs a great deal of repetition and practice. Repetition and practice are essential keys to learning; however, it is equally essential that they not be dull.

For the student who is able to read a book, even at a level lower than expected for her age and grade, the best practice at every lesson is having the student read to herself "easy" books that she selects. Reading for pleasure helps develop fluency and confidence; both are important underpinnings for reading more difficult books.

You will be very pleased when your student reads a new sound or word correctly for the first time, but you cannot assume that therefore she has learned it. The student should practice the new skill for a few minutes in every session for weeks, until she knows it automatically without having to think about it. Then it is important to review regularly to make sure that she remembers. A skill or a bit of knowledge, if not used, is easily forgotten.

On the other hand, it is also important not to reach the point of boredom. As soon as you are satisfied that her knowledge is automatic, the special practice can be dropped. A good rule of thumb is that if the student recognizes the new sound or word without thinking about it for three weeks in a row, then she has really learned it.

To prevent necessary repetition and practice from becoming dull, keep practice sessions brief and crisp. Have your student:

- practice the same skill in a variety of ways.
- learn to recognize a word by practicing/writing it, reading it and forming it with a variety of materials.
- search for examples of the word in newspapers and magazines, play games that include the word and learn to recognize it on flash cards.

- **Cut down on distractions as much as possible.**

- Try to find a place that is relatively quiet. It is impossible to eliminate all noise, and it is unnecessary to do so.

- Make sure that you eliminate as many visual distractions as possible. Keep the table clear of materials that you are not using at the moment.

- If you must work with the student near a window or a door, have her sit with her back to it so that she will not see people, animals or vehicles pass by.

- If you work in a room where there are other students, place a partition, such as a bookcase or a screen, between your student and others. If this is difficult, she can sit with her back to the others.

Many students are easily distracted by things that you would not notice if you were concentrating on something specific. The sound of a fire engine, a buzzing fly, a moving object or another student can draw attention away from the work at hand. To make it easier to concentrate during the session, find a spot where you can interact with the fewest possibilities of distraction.

Realistically, the physical conditions in which you will be working are often less than perfect. It may be noisy, the light may be poor and there may not be a chalkboard; you may even have to find yourself a different corner each week. Depending on the nature of the program, particularly if you are working with a group of students, you may not be able to do much about some of these conditions. Do the best you can.

Remember that your goal is to make it easier for the student to concentrate on her work. Sometimes even the material on the page distracts her from the very word or line that she is reading. Some students find it easier to concentrate on one word or line if all the others are covered. Use a ruler, a sheet of paper or a page mask to help the student focus only on the material that is relevant at the moment.

Try not to compromise on these points:

- Assure an older student absolute privacy away from young children.

- Try to use the same location for each lesson.

- Arrange to have enough light, particularly for the student.

- **Make decisions simple by limiting the number of choices.**

Most of us have difficulty making decisions. To make it easier for your student to decide between alternatives, it is advisable to offer only two or three possibilities. Instead of asking, "What would you like to do next?" try, "Would you like to play tic-tac-toe or Go Fish?" Instead of asking, "What would you like to do tomorrow?" try, "Would you like to go to the museum or take a trip to the park?"

In the first type of question, the possibilities are endless, making the choice difficult for the student. Furthermore, he may choose something impractical or unrealistic, which you may not be able to accommodate. By offering only a few options, you make the selection simpler for him and guarantee that either one is possible. You are also indicating that you respect him by accepting his decision.

• **Plan for success; if the student fails, your plan needs improvement.**

It is very important for your student to experience success. As he learns one skill successfully, he will be encouraged to approach the next with confidence. In order to achieve success as early as possible, it is important to plan an instructional program in which each new unit is small. Each unit must present a challenge, but one that is within his current grasp.

If the student fails to learn the new material, plan your lesson again. Try a new approach. Analyze the task in order to present smaller steps to the student. The following example provides an illustration of the small steps involved in learning a simple task—in this case, how to prepare a soft-boiled egg. You might break down the task into these steps:

1. Remove the egg carton from the refrigerator.

2. Remove one egg from the carton, placing it in a bowl so that it will not roll off the table.

3. Close carton securely, and return it to the refrigerator.

4. Remove a small saucepan from the storage cabinet.

5. Pour enough water into the saucepan to cover the egg.

6. Place the saucepan on the stove.

7. Turn on the burner and adjust it to medium heat.

8. Heat the water until it is bubbling gently.

9. Carefully place the egg into the hot water with a tablespoon.

10. Lower the heat.

11. When the water begins to simmer, set the timer for three minutes.

12. Turn off the heat when the timer rings.

13. Remove the egg from the saucepan with a spoon and place it in the bowl with cold water to cool slightly.

14. When the shell is cool enough to handle, crack it open and spoon the cooked egg into a dish.

Here the steps have been made very small so that you understand how a task may be broken down for the learner who needs such guidance. In some instances, a task may be broken down into steps that are a bit larger, but still helpful.

- **Reward success.**

Let the student know when he has succeeded, even with a very small task, and celebrate that success. A reward can take many forms: it can be a smile; a hearty response, such as, "That was great, John"; a piece of candy, a cookie or a star; or a credit that is later traded in for a prize. As the student has more successes, he will need fewer rewards and will derive more pleasure from successful learning. Eventually, the pleasure of learning will be the only reward he needs. In the meantime, it is important to acknowledge success.

It is just as important to acknowledge and compliment the student for trying, even when he is unsuccessful. But do not compliment the student on success when he has not really achieved it. While an instructor may sometimes do this to encourage the student, it does not have the desired effect. Students know when they have not been successful, and will recognize that the instructor is not being honest and straightforward.

- **Teach at the student's level.**

When anyone is asked to do work that is beyond their abilities they are bound to encounter serious problems. Finding the correct level at which a student should be taught is one of your most important challenges. If a student is struggling in the fifth grade a teacher might try to be helpful by giving him a third-grade "reader." Unfortunately, this material may also be gibberish to him. In doing this, the teacher has not realized that the student is able to read only a few words and does not yet know that he must read across the page from left to right. Unless the instruction starts at the student's actual level, whatever it is, the student will not progress.

The student's level will vary depending on which skill you happen to be observing at the moment. Evaluate his skills, helping him learn those that he lacks while recognizing and making use of his strengths.

- **Respect the privacy of confidential information.**

You will be privileged to know many things about your student that should be kept confidential. Under no circumstances is it permissible to chat or gossip about a student's private concerns. The only person with whom information may be shared is the director of the program, the guidance counselor or the principal.

Confidential information can be particularly embarrassing to the student when he has personal contact with your family. For this reason, it is best to avoid working with a student who is a friend of your child or a child of your friend.

- **Listen and do not criticize.**

To save time, the instructor may try to help a student by interrupting her presentation to criticize and correct. It is far more constructive to listen patiently, without criticism and with as few suggestions as possible. A friendly, sympathetic listener is more helpful than a well-meaning critic and director. There must be no suggestion of criticism of the adult or child who does not read well. Criticism can destroy self-confidence and interest in learning; do not shame the student, and never, ever be sarcastic.

The manner in which you react to errors is also very important. When the student has made an error, correct it casually, rather than emphasize her mistake by asking questions to lead her to correct herself. State the rule instead of asking. If it is appropriate, teach and re-teach the point, but do not make an issue of the error itself.

Many of your students will speak English with an accent. Remember, your primary purpose is to teach reading. Too many corrections of her speech can be interpreted by the student as criticism and can destroy her interest in learning. Limit your corrections to those that affect the meaning of words. This is a very subtle and difficult point: it is essential to correct only important errors. Concentrate on helping her understand what she reads in English. If you feel, however, that the student's speech is a serious handicap, then you should inquire about having a speech specialist evaluate the problem. But you will not be helping your student if you step into that area in addition to reading.

Notes for Tutors & Teacher Assistants

- **Maintain a professional relationship with the student.**

Your relationship with the student should be friendly, respectful and professional! However, it is helpful to keep some distance, so that you can retain your privacy and she can retain hers. The student may share some intimate thoughts and private information with you, but you should never pry or ask her for such information. When it comes up, let it be because she wishes to share, and trusts that you will keep it confidential.

Never break an appointment without notifying the student. Arrange to have your student call the office if she must be late or miss an appointment. This will encourage her to feel a responsibility to you and the program. But do not be too disappointed if she breaks an appointment or fails to call. If a student is absent, find out why; a telephone call or a home visit may help. She may be afraid to return if she thinks that she has stayed away too long. When she returns, inquire about her health, but do not reproach her.

Never forget that you are not a magician. You cannot straighten out your student's marital problems, or help her family make ends meet, or get her what she wants for Christmas or find her the job that she desires. When you are confronted with problems that give you concern and that you feel someone should do something about, discuss them with your supervisor.

- **Maintain a professional relationship with the classroom teacher.**

The teacher is responsible for the student while she is at school. He may feel frustrated and helpless because the student has failed to make progress or is difficult to manage in the classroom. At the same time, he is overwhelmed by the problem of helping this student while trying to deal with the whole class. Nevertheless, the arrival of a new person who may be more successful with the student can sometimes cause the teacher to feel threatened. The tutor must be courteous to the teacher, respect his professionalism and understand the difficulty of trying to teach thirty or more students at once. It is important to remember that in dealing with students one-to-one or in small groups outside the classroom, the tutor has a far simpler job than the teacher, and in no way competes with him. The tutor serves as "supplementary" personnel—helping the teacher accomplish what he has no time to do by himself. When this relationship is maintained, teachers find that having such assistance enables them to teach more effectively, and they are happy about the progress made by students who receive supplementary help. They become enthusiastic about the program and are eager for it to continue from year to year.

Under no circumstance should supplementary assistance be imposed on a teacher; only teachers who request assistance should receive it.

- **Maintain a professional relationship with the principal, your supervisor and other school personnel.**

The staff of your tutorial program are working together to help solve the problem of illiteracy. Some have more experience and training than you; some may have less. But remember, all of you are working together as a team.

You may wonder about things you see being done or not being done. Ask questions of the person responsible, keeping an open mind:

- Try to avoid jumping to conclusions.
- Try to avoid being destructively critical and stirring up tempests.
- Remember that everyone involved is trying and that no one way of doing things has been proven to be the best.
- Be tolerant of a certain degree of disorganization.
- Accept the fact that there are problems.
- When you have questions about techniques and problems in relation to a particular case, ask for assistance. Such requests reflect your sincere effort and interest and will earn you the respect of the staff.

When working in a school or an agency that hosts a tutorial program, it is important to be helpful and, at the same time, invisible. The principal, teachers and assistants are all very busy, and at first they may seem to ignore you, assuming that you already know your way around. They are glad that you're there, but they may forget to tell you some of the little details that would make life a bit easier for you.

Be sure you know where the important features of the school are located, such as the principal's office, the lavatories, the telephones, the fire exits and the library. The school will provide places for you to work, hang your coat and keep your books, lesson plans and other materials.

Try to impose as little as possible on regular school personnel in the beginning. Although supplementary tutors are a great help, every extra person in the building adds a burden to the regular staff because each one needs space, supplies and a host of little things. Try to make that burden as light as possible; for example, bring magazines from home instead of asking the school to get them. Leave the furniture as you find it, store your materials where you can find them easily (preferably in the space provided), clear away any scrap paper and try not to use the school telephone. Soon you will be able to do things and find things for yourself, and as time goes on, your work will go a lot more smoothly and your contribution will be better appreciated.

- **Maintain a professional relationship with parents.**

The relationship between the tutor and the student's family should be courteous but impersonal. The tutor's primary relationship and loyalty is with the student. If the tutor reports to a parent or other family member, the relationship with the student will be endangered. If a parent asks the tutor for a report on the student's progress or wishes to discuss the child with the tutor, the parent should be referred to the person who coordinates the program at the school.

The classroom teacher is responsible for discussing the student's progress with the parent. Parent conferences may be arranged in which the classroom and the tutorial programs are described and discussed. Discussions about individual students, however, should be restricted to special conferences arranged by the supervisor or coordinator. Even when the student is receiving private instruction, the tutor's primary loyalty is to the student.

- **Maintain your professionalism at home.**

Never discuss the problems of your students with your family or friends. Protecting the trust of your student is something you need to do even when you've gone home.

- **Maintain an awareness of the student as an individual.**

Your shining goal is to help the student become self-motivated. The acquisition of reading skills is just one step in becoming a whole person. Although your contact with the student revolves around reading, your instruction, because it is so individualized, affects his total behavior. As his attitude toward learning changes, there will be changes in his entire personality. It is not an exaggeration to say that in these changes lie your—and his—greatest accomplishment.

Be certain that older students are protected from the prying and sometimes unkind eyes of young children, who may ridicule them because they require remedial instruction or because they are learning "baby" work.

- **Help your student set realistic goals.**

While setting higher goals for your student, help him maintain a realistic evaluation of his strengths and limitations. An eighteen-year-old boy who reads at the second-grade level must continue to aspire to improve his reading, but it is not generally helpful for him to expect to become a doctor.

- **Be confident that your student will learn.**

When the teacher expects a student to learn, she will tend to learn quite well. If the teacher is forewarned that the student is dull, and therefore anticipates that she will not learn easily, the student will again meet the teacher's expectations, and fail to learn as well as she might. There is a magical quality in a teacher's expectations; the learner tends to succeed or fail accordingly.

Have confidence that your students will learn!

- **Be patient; don't be rushed. This is a long haul.**

You and your student must understand that learning can be rapid, or it can be a long, slow struggle. Progress may be so slow that you may feel as though there is no movement at all. You cannot hope to teach overnight what your student has failed for years to learn. For this reason, it is important to keep records of exactly where the student was at the beginning of instruction—so that you may make a more realistic evaluation of her progress.

Progress may be slow for a long period of time, and then suddenly there will be a breakthrough. Hopefully, that will happen when you are still working with the student, and you will have the pleasure of seeing her speed ahead. Sometimes the breakthrough comes long afterward and you may hear of it years later or never learn about it at all. In either case, your student will have come closer to realizing her goal.

Summary of the Principles of Teaching and Learning

To summarize, here are the high points to remember about teaching:

 The teacher must understand that:

- each student is unique.

- each student learns at a different rate.

- every student can learn. If a student has not learned, she has been poorly taught.

- there is no single method of teaching that works for all students. Learning to read for the first time is difficult for many.

- if the student has already failed, remedial work is a long, slow path. Much of it seems like marking time. Be patient.

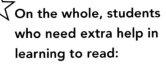 **On the whole, students who need extra help in learning to read:**

- feel stupid, though it may not be apparent.

- may be restless.

- may have a brief attention span.

- may be easily distracted.

- need to learn through all their senses, rather than only through seeing and hearing.

- may have poor handwriting.

- may have difficulty focusing, and therefore understanding what they hear or see.

- may quickly forget what they are taught.

- need lots of repetition and practice.

- may have difficulty understanding words that represent concepts.

- may interpret expressions literally.

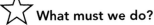 **What must we do?**

- Find out what interests the student, and use these interests as a lever for learning.

- Accentuate the positive; overlook the negative.

- Praise the student for learning. Lack of praise makes the student indifferent to behaving properly.

- Never be sarcastic.

- Avoid reproaches.

- Aim to develop joy in learning.

- Don't lecture. Don't moralize.

- Be consistent, kind and firm.

- Set rules and routines, and provide structure. The student will welcome knowing what to expect.

- Remember that no problem is too small to work with, and to work with slowly.

- Don't bite off too much at one time.

- Overteach every skill until it has become automatic.

- If the student has failures, plan smaller units. You may be asking too much of her at this point.

- Use varied and colorful materials, and a multi-sensory approach.

- Plan many activities within each session. Change from one activity to another before the student tires.

- Keep in mind that individuals differ in their learning styles.

- Minimize noise and clutter where you meet with the student.

- Provide whatever assistance the student needs.

- Use simple language.

- Do not talk down to the student.

- Do not criticize his language.

- Accept him as he is.

- Establish realistic expectations and make reasonable demands (simple at first, then more difficult) so that the student will have a chance to feel successful.

- Assign learning tasks that are at the appropriate level but difficult enough to provide a challenge.

- Remember that the student's profile of skills is probably uneven; she will exhibit different levels in different areas.

- Compare the student's progress with her own record, not with other students'.

- Make decisions easier for the student by limiting choices and asking not "What do you want?" but "Do you want this or that?"

- Maintain a sense of humor.

Part I

Chapter 4: Tips on Techniques

Specific Aids and Resources

Printing

Beginning readers find it easier to read printed letters that are large, consistent and presented in lines with ample space between them. You should therefore work with manuscript printing, which is used in the early elementary grades.

This is manuscript printing.

Be sure that you print each letter clearly and consistently. Since the beginning reader has great difficulty in distinguishing one letter from another, ordinary handwriting may add to his confusion.

Everyday penmanship is called cursive writing, or script. It is usually taught in the third grade.

This is cursive writing

Students will pick up cursive writing quickly once they have mastered the basic reading skills.

Files

Prepare a folder for each student. This is her portfolio. Keep all of the student's work neatly arranged in the folder. If you are working with a young child, suggest that she make a drawing on the cover to personalize her folder; she should be encouraged to feel proud of the work in this portfolio. The student may read to you her writing from the folder, and at the end of the semester, you may send home samples of her work so that she can share her accomplishments with family and friends.

Also prepare an individual file of cards for each student containing new words or words that the student finds difficult. Using a felt-tip pen or a heavy crayon, print one word on each card. Separate the cards into three groups: those she knows well (these are *Friends*), those she does not know (these are *Strangers*), and those she may know at times but still needs to practice (these are *Acquaintances*). If possible, obtain a metal or wood box in which the student can maintain her file. Have her file the *Friends* alphabetically. Practice for a few minutes at each lesson, so that some of the *Acquaintances* can be added to the *Friends* file and some of the *Strangers* to the *Acquaintances* file. The movement of each word into the *Friends* file represents a real achievement for the learner.

Notebooks

The student should have a hardcover notebook, in which she is encouraged to work neatly and take pride. If your student cannot carry her notebook home or if she has no homework assignment, keep it in the folder between lessons. Some teachers have been very successful in having students practice on loose paper and rewrite beautifully in the notebook, which then becomes part of the portfolio and a source of increased pride.

About the Lesson

Know what you are planning to do during each lesson. Try to limit each activity to five minutes.

A sample plan might include the following activities:

- Present a new concept.

- Review and practice consonant blends, or words that were *Acquaintances* at the last lesson.

- Discuss an upcoming trip to a museum to see Egyptian mummies or a TV show that he watched the previous evening.

- Write about plans for the trip or the TV show. Encourage the student to write this on his own; ignore spelling errors. If he is unable to write the story, have him dictate to you.

- Have him read back the story, learn the words, and add the appropriate ones to his file of *Friends* words.

- Read from a book chosen by the student, perhaps continued from a previous lesson.

- Read to the student an anecdote, a funny story or a newspaper item that you saved to share.

- Play a word game, if there is time.

See page 161 for sample lesson plan.

These suggestions, described in greater detail below, are easily adaptable for individual, small group or classroom use:

1. Teach something new at the beginning of each lesson.

Introduce something new to maintain the student's interest. At the end of the lesson, it is very helpful to summarize what was done that day. Include some mention of each new achievement: a word learned, a story read, a fact clarified.

It is important to review the latest skills taught until you are confident that the student knows them well and is not likely to forget them. Do not assume that your student remembers what he was taught during previous sessions. Your notes on each lesson will tell you which of the skills covered last time should be reviewed today, and today's notes will remind you of what needs to be reviewed at the next session. Include a five-minute review in some part of the session.

2. Check your student's work.

Read all the written work your student does during the lesson. Do not rely on comparing his answers with those on answer sheets provided by some publishers. A great deal of the student's progress is a result of the personal relationship you have established with him. When you check his work, you quickly become aware of his errors, and are in a position to clear up areas of confusion immediately. An answer sheet cannot substitute for you.

3. Read aloud.

Spend several minutes of each session reading to your student from a book in which the student is interested, but that is above his reading level. Difficulty in learning to read does not preclude having experience and understanding in many other areas of life. For this reason, it is important to remember that for adults and children, interest and comprehension are usually beyond reading ability. Discuss the reading material with him. By doing this, you are giving him pleasant associations with the printed word and encouraging self-expression, an important corollary of reading skill.

4. Encourage your student to read with you.

If your student is reluctant to read aloud to you, take turns reading aloud with her. Be cautious about criticizing even slight reading errors during the early phases of instruction. Since your goal is to encourage relaxation and reduce self-consciousness, such criticism is likely to inhibit the student. Should she have difficulty with a word, supply it. If she has difficulty with too many words, the material you are reading is too difficult. Shift to an easier selection.

In addition, have the student read silently at times, absorbing the text and enjoying the illustrations on her own. After she has read it, let her tell you about it.

5. Engage your student in conversation.

Encourage oral expression and create a relaxed teaching atmosphere by discussing favorite television shows with your student. Assign a show of particular interest to her, have her describe the show and discuss it with her. Discuss magazine pictures, current events and newspaper stories as well.

6. Keep notes.

At the end of each lesson, make a note in your folder of what you did and your immediate thoughts on what you want to do next time. Do not rely on your memory. Also note anything that the student said or did that you want to discuss with your supervisor. In some programs, the supervisor may provide a form for filling out these reports. If a form is not provided, staple sheets of paper for recording notes to the inside cover of your folder. Always remember to date your entry. When the sheet is full, do not turn it over; staple another sheet over it, with the staples at the top of the sheet, so that you can more easily leaf through the notes.

7. Have students help students.

If you should be tutoring several students at a time, you may find it helpful to have some of the students assist others so that you can work with an individual. When such assignments are judiciously made and carefully supervised, this can work out well.

8. Assign homework carefully.

There is no hard-and-fast rule about assigning homework. Avoid giving homework if it is likely to destroy a student's interest in the instruction. If he asks for homework, give him an assignment, and be sure to check it when he turns it in. He will be very disappointed if you forget, and may fail to do the work the next time. Do not reproach him if he has not done it, and do not assign more until he requests it.

Homework must be handled sensitively not only by the instructor but also by the classroom teacher, who must be creative in assigning homework that addresses the varying interests and the wide range of skills among her students.

9. More Ideas

The following techniques will encourage your student to express herself and learn to enjoy the printed word:

- Send your student notes, letters or written messages.

- Help her keep a journal, a notebook or a diary of thoughts and ideas.

- Tape-record a book as you read it aloud so that the student can hear it again and again.

- Encourage her, when appropriate, to create posters, models, dioramas or puppets for special occasions.

- Encourage your student to compose original stories.

- Read to or with her at each session.

- Talk with your student about things that are important to her.

Additional Resources And Techniques

1. Libraries

The public library is an invaluable source of material for a reading program. Once the librarian is familiar with your needs, she will be happy to locate appropriate materials for you. She can provide interesting books and periodicals that you might not otherwise find. Libraries also have computer and internet access for students who may not have them at home. Take your student to the library if you can, and help him register for a library card. You may find that he will be very proud to own a library card of his own.

Your student may ask to borrow books from the program or the classroom; if you can spare the books, it is worth lending them. Again, do not reproach the student if he does not return the book. Ask for it once and no more; if a student fails to return a borrowed book, do not lend another.

2. Printed Materials

If tabloid newspapers, comic books and picture magazines appeal to your student, use them as tools to teach critical evaluation of reading material. They can be very helpful in motivating your student to enjoy reading and to experience success at his present level of instruction.

3. Field Trips

Plan to take your student to places he has never visited, preferably where the admission is free. Exciting destinations for field trips include museums, a theater, monuments, historic buildings, a park, a firehouse and a ferryboat. You will be surprised at how much these outings will mean to your student.

Such visits should not replace regular instruction too often. Discuss the visit in advance, emphasizing what to look for and expect. Afterward, have your students discuss the visit with you and write a story about it or dictate one to you. Focus on the pleasures of the visit and the excitement of discovering something wonderful nearby. Take care to avoid making the afterwork feel like an unpleasant burden.

4. Environmental Literacy

Encourage your student (especially a beginning reader) to read signs everywhere: highway signs, street signs, signs on TV, advertising signs and labels and signs at work and at school. Cut advertisements out of magazines. Boys may be particularly interested in automobile names and in traffic signs such as STOP and DETOUR. If a student is interested, encourage him to make a file of these signs, treating them as you do the word file, that is, as *Friends*, *Strangers* and *Acquaintances*.

5. Fun Materials

Having the student use such materials as felt-tip pens, Magic Markers, crayons and colored pencils adds variety and interest to written work.

6. Workbooks

To make your printed material go further and to make it easier to select exactly what you want, you will find it helpful to remove the pages of a workbook or a book of reading exercises. Staple each page to a sheet of oak tag or stiff cardboard, then file the sheets in a filing cabinet or a carton. Use each sheet of practice material as needed, and then replace it in the file.

This practice allows maximum utilization of a limited amount of teaching material, and has the added advantage of discouraging dependence on any one workbook, which would be of limited value to the student. Be careful not to let workbook exercises substitute for teaching.

If you do not have enough books to use in this way, and a photocopier is not available to you, use transparent material, such as tracing paper or a sheet of clear acetate, to cover the page you wish to use; have the student write his answers on the transparent material, so that the book remains clean. (If you use clear plastic sheets, the student can write with a dry erase marker that can be wiped off.)

7. Role-Playing

An excellent way to encourage self-expression is to dramatize different situations. Role-playing is an interesting and effective activity for all age groups. Although it may be more exciting when done with a group, it can also be managed very nicely in individual instruction, with both the instructor and the student participating. The enjoyment and usefulness of role-playing is enhanced by the use of everyday props such as pads, pencils, clocks and telephones. For example, by playacting a situation that involves a telephone, the student will gain confidence with a critical skill. Some students are uncomfortable speaking on the phone and avoid doing it, while others find it easier than addressing a person directly. In both cases, practicing phone conversations encourages self-expression.

Other situations and relationships may be dramatized to beneficial effect. You and your student may address some of her concerns by playing the roles of a parent and a child, a job interviewer and an applicant, a salesperson and a shopper or a government official and a citizen.

In role-playing with children, the use of hand puppets adds variety and color to the drama. Inexpensive puppets may be purchased, or the child can make them herself by drawing figures on paper bags or old socks with a permanent marker.

8. Technology

Working on a computer with your student stimulates interest and adds variety to the lesson. It also allows a student who may be uncomfortable with computers to gain confidence in using one. Have the student type his own story on the computer, or dictate to you. A tape or digital recorder can be used to record the student's progress in oral reading or to record discussions and stories; students learn a lot by listening to themselves, and usually enjoy it.

9. Games

Playing games takes the monotony and drudgery out of the practice necessary for success. The best games are often homemade, but there are many commercial games that are useful in teaching. In games of skill, you will more often be the winner at the beginning. In games of chance, where the moves depend on a spinner or the roll of dice, the players have an equal chance of winning. Even though he is eager to win, and you would like him to win, play fair; he will know if you yield the game, and it will not help his self-esteem. It is best to avoid competitive games; adapt the games of skill so that both players try to beat their last score. This way, the student competes with himself rather than with the other players.

10. Popular Media

Your student is exposed to many forms of electronic media every day. These experiences can serve as the basis for discussions that will guide him toward thinking critically about his favorite music videos, computer games, films and TV shows. Have the student:

- describe the sequence of events: what happened and when.
- explain why the performance was interesting.
- select the most important sections.
- analyze why the protagonist did what she did.
- consider alternative outcomes for the story.
- explain what was good or bad about the show or game.

This kind of discussion can help develop analytical and critical thinking skills far beyond the level at which the student is able to read.

11. Computer Programs

Computer games or instructional programs may or may not be helpful to your student. Before you use a computer game or program during a lesson, try it yourself and then consider its suitability. Some computer software series can be great motivators for students, and incorporate serious learning activities in games that appeal to children and youngsters, e.g. Knowledge Adventure *Jumpstart* series.

- Do you have all the equipment required for this game?
- Is the program at the right level for your student?
- Does it provide a challenge?
- Is the challenge too great and therefore frustrating?
- Is the program too speedy? Is it too slow?
- Does it give feedback on correct answers and errors?

Conclusion

You will have successes and failures with various techniques. You may be discouraged by your student's lack of progress; you may feel that you have been unable to make a connection with him; you may feel uncomfortable around him. All of these problems arise even for the best and most experienced of teachers. These problems do not necessarily reflect on you; ask your supervisor for advice on how to deal with them. If you are working in a team setting where a counselor, a psychologist or a psychiatrist is available, you may, at times, wish to request an evaluation of a student by other specialists.

When you feel that you have not made a connection or feel uncomfortable, you may request that the student be transferred to another instructor. For similar reasons, a student may be transferred to you.

Concern about failures and lack of progress is the daily lot of the good teacher. Should you feel such concern, your supervisor will assist you with new materials and techniques, or will reassure you.

NOTES

Teach Anyone To Read: The No-Nonsense Guide

Part I

Chapter 5: Schoolchildren

Pre-school Through Middle School

Most of the following suggestions have been discussed in previous chapters, and are relevant to working with learners of all ages. However, they are particularly important when working with children. Be patient; the repetition is important.

Trips are very important.

Outings to the zoo or an animal farm, a museum, the library or a firehouse will expand a child's experience and vocabulary.

Associate reading with pleasure.

Read to the child for a few minutes each day, and playact the story with her. This will encourage self-expression and fun in learning.

Use games as part of the instruction.

In the course of enjoying educational games (i.e., board games, computer games), the child learns reading skills. Do not feel impatient because the games take a long time to play. The pleasure associated with the instruction time and the satisfaction derived from every correct move are positive gains for the child.

Spend time having fun with words.

Make rhymes, read nonsense poems and play word games, such as the naming game that begins, "A—my name is Alice and my husband's name is Allan; we come from Alabama and we live on Amity Street." Play "Geography." These activities give a child practice in listening to the sounds of words, an important skill in learning to read.

Notes for Tutors & Teacher Assistants

Provide fresh materials.

Use different textbooks and workbooks for supplementary instruction from those used in the child's regular classroom.

Evaluate the child's reading level.

Do not assume that the child is at the reading level expected for her age or grade. The earlier the evaluation is done, the sooner the child can be given instruction that will be helpful to her. (See Chapter 14, "Estimating Your Student's Reading Level.")

Be aware of the child's school environment.

Discuss with your supervisor whether it would be appropriate to meet with the child's classroom teacher to discuss common goals.

Consider your student's physical comfort

If the child is being tutored after school, find out if it is possible to provide a light snack before or during your session. A snack is a pleasant and comforting way to start a session, as well as a way to make sure that hunger pangs will not divert your student's attention.

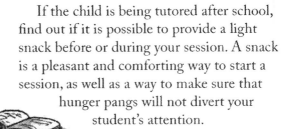

Use rewards when appropriate.

Small, inexpensive rewards, such as a ball, rubber stamps, marbles, stickers or a book, are wonderful incentives and help form positive associations with the learning experience. These should not be viewed as bribes, but rather as a celebration of success. As the instruction progresses, the need for these incentives will disappear; learning will become its own reward. On occasion, a child will ask for "presents" even when she has not earned any. It must be explained simply and clearly that the prizes are rewards that are given only when earned. When the instructor is consistent, firm and pleasant, children will accept the rules graciously.

The cost of these rewards, and the snacks mentioned above, should be borne by the school or the program.

Use variety and pacing.

Prepare many different activities for each lesson; before the child wearies of one activity, it is wise to shift to another.

Allow breaks from sitting quietly.

Introduce occasional opportunities for the child to move around: to get a drink of water or to play Simple Simon for a few minutes before returning to a new table activity.

Don't get angry when problems arise.

Some children who present behavior problems at school will try to "test" you while getting to know you. Such behavior is best handled without reproach, but with firm, gentle reminders of what is acceptable and what the rules are.

Students may come late, or come on time but refuse to do the work or use language that is meant to shock. If the child is not ready to settle down for a one-to-one lesson, it may be helpful to suspend formal instruction for the day with a reminder that you plan to teach him at the next session, when he is ready to work. Review your plan for the session to make sure that the activities are varied enough to capture the child's attention and cooperation more fully.

Teach Anyone To Read: The No-Nonsense Guide

Chapter 6: Adolescents and Adults

Working with Older Students

> Non-reading teenagers are more common than you might think, both in New York City and the affluent communities that surround it. The less fortunate ones end up jobless and in prison. The lucky ones get taken into...schools that build their reading skills from scratch and send many of them on to college.
>
> Brent Staples
> *The New York Times*, 8/25/02

Even though dropouts have failed academically and may consider themselves stupid, they are often desperately eager to learn. When some of them dropped out of school, they were still certain that they could succeed in the outside world. They tried, and many found the experience bitter. Jobs are difficult to get, and low-paying, dead-end jobs are often demanding, boring and menial.

Often enough, dropouts are unemployed and unhappy about it. Perhaps someone has persuaded them to try school once more to gain the tools necessary for better opportunities. In a sense, when such an individual comes to you, he is challenging your program: "No teacher was ever able to teach me before. Do you think you can do better?" You will have to rise to this challenge. Until now, no one has given him enough individual attention, set achievable goals or shown real commitment to his success. With gentle, firm reassurance, you can build his self-confidence and help him learn.

2. Motivation

Some of your students come involuntarily: your goal is to motivate them to want to learn without regard for the reasons that they are in the program. Sometimes they receive a stipend for attending a reading program, and it is reduced if they do not attend. These students present a great challenge, since learning requires more than attendance: it requires interest, motivation and confidence that one can learn and that it is worthwhile to invest effort in learning.

3. Age-Appropriate Materials

Be sure to seek out or create material of interest to adults. If you have to use material designed for children, adults will usually accept it if you explain that it is all that is available, but since the material is only a tool, even this can be helpful. As soon as possible, bring in material that is more suitable for adults.

4. Privacy

For older students, privacy is essential; make sure they are never taught where younger children can observe them. Also, it may be embarrassing to an older student to carry a book that is obviously at a low reading level; cover the book with a college book jacket.

5. Independent Reading

As soon as the student is ready for supplementary reading, lend him a book. He may be surprised by the pride he feels when he walks through the streets carrying a book that he is reading with success. This pride is a great incentive.

6. Useful Goals

If the student's reading level is between the fourth and ninth grades, relate the reading instruction to vocational goals. For example, if a young man is interested in being an auto mechanic, find manuals, instructional guides and books about cars and mechanics to support and maintain his interest.

If his reading level is at the ninth grade or higher, set a goal of earning the GED, or high school equivalency certificate. Call the local high school for information about the examination for this certificate. Plan your instruction in relation to the examination requirements. The certificate has prestige as well as vocational and college-entrance value. It is an important goal.

7. Respect for Students

Avoid making references to school grades and to levels of ability. Have each student compete with his own record, not with that of other students.

Remember that even adults who are not yet able to read have a wide range of experience and a relatively full vocabulary. Your tone, language and materials offered should reflect respect for your student's non-academic achievements, as well as for the courage and fortitude it took to return to the school environment.

8. Emphasize Skills and Strengths

You have much to learn from your adult students, who have skills, intelligence and information in many areas where you may not. Discussions and "brainstorming" in areas of mutual interest (such as current events or community problems) are invaluable adjuncts of reading instruction; they encourage oral expression, sharpen thinking skills and build self-confidence.

9. Maturity and Confidence

Adults will be responsive to instruction, provided that they are treated with courtesy, respect and praise for achievement, and without reproaches. Adults can discipline themselves, stick to a job and work hard at it, if they see results. They will do homework if they feel they are learning something useful.

Adults who have never had the opportunity to learn to read have not experienced failure in school and, therefore, may not have suffered as much emotional damage as have dropouts. Still, their academic self-esteem may be low. They are aware of their great handicap in daily life and in vocational competence. They fear failure, and suspect that they may be "too dumb" or too old to learn. These students will have many doubts and hesitations. You must address their doubts and hesitations and convince them that they can improve their reading skills, and that in doing so, they will improve their lives immeasurably.

NOPQRSTUV
WXYZABCDE
FGHIJKLMN
OPQRSTUVW
XYZABCDEF
GHIJKLMNO
PQRSTUVWX
YZABCDEFG
HIJKLMNOPQ
RSTUVWXYZ

Part II

Working with Students for Whom English Is a Second Language

Part II

Cultural Background

Did you know that, for 32 million Americans over the age of five, English is a second language? This was the report of the 1990 Census. As you read these words, the figure is undoubtedly larger, for the number of immigrants has increased rapidly since the 1990 census. This figure does not include illegal immigrants, who are uncounted. Spanish is the most common first language; the Asian language population shows the most rapid rise (Chinese, Tagalog, Korean, Vietnamese, Japanese, Thai, Mon-Khmer), as does the French Creole. German, Italian, Polish, Greek, Yiddish, Hungarian, and Dutch were spoken less frequently at home in 1990 than in 1980.

For many of your students, English is a second language. Their native tongue may be Spanish, Navajo, Turkish, Italian, Russian or Chinese. Some students understand no English at all, while others understand much of what they hear, but speak haltingly and are unable to read. Some recent immigrants live in communities where only their native language is spoken. Although your area of responsibility is reading, with this group of students it must be expanded to include speech.

To learn to read English, the foreign-speaking student needs to acquire some listening and speaking skills in this language. Therefore, the first phase of instruction must concentrate on the acquisition of oral language skills, including the development of vocabulary and the ability to hold a conversation. As with all students, the foreign-speaking individual must be encouraged to speak, with corrections limited to major errors.

The challenge of learning English as a second language (ESL) is quite special. Because the student must learn to speak English before or while she learns to read it, and is at the same time adjusting to a new way of life, it will be extremely hard for her to meet the demands of the work. Therefore, teaching ESL requires an understanding of and sensitivity to your student's cultural background in order to help her achieve her goals.

To understand the student's behavior and attitude you will have to know a good deal about the world of the student. The more you know about her culture and values—her habits, routines and family ties; what is considered important and unimportant; and which behaviors are considered proper and commendable and which are considered bad—the better able you will be to communicate clearly with her.

Cultural differences have made this country vital and dynamic. Do not sit in judgment of the student's world and the ways in which it may differ from your own background and values. Understand that your student developed her behavior patterns in a different environment, with different cultural practices. Now that she has been transplanted into what is, for her, a strange world, her values may change, and so may yours. But these changes must be a natural result of the exchange between student and instructor.

Sometimes a student's attitude may be disconcerting or distressing to you. It is important to reserve judgment; you may learn that such behavior can be interpreted as completely acceptable in view of her cultural background. As an example, punctuality is highly valued in mainstream American industrialized society, and less valued in places where there is little industry. Although it is inconvenient when a student is late for an appointment, you must be able to recognize when this apparently cavalier attitude toward time is part of a cultural pattern and not intended as a personal affront.

In many countries, sex roles are more sharply contrasted than in the United States. Quite often, the man is the absolute head of the family. He earns the living and makes all of the decisions, while the woman takes care of the home and is constrained to be more passive. In preparation for their adult roles, children play games that anticipate the behavior expected of them as adults; hence, boys must not play sissy games and girls may not play rough games. Although these patterns are changing, the cultural contrast remains striking.

Many students from immigrant families are embarrassed and insecure because of the difference between the languages spoken and behaviors expected at home and at school. This can contribute to failure in school. The student who feels isolated in an unfriendly, English-speaking world, surrounded by people who look down at those she loves, tends to feel more comfortable speaking only her native language with her own group. She may have failed to learn English for these reasons.

You must demonstrate in your behavior and speech that you respect your student and her culture. You should communicate clearly your belief that she is a worthy individual and your confidence in her ability to learn. An invaluable way to demonstrate your respect is to be able to converse with the student in her native language. If you don't know her language, ask her to teach you some common words and phrases. This provides a double benefit: you form a bond with the student and acquire a smattering of another language.

Teach Anyone To Read: The No-Nonsense Guide

Chapter 8: Learning English as a Second Language

English as a Special Challenge

Learning a second language can be as easy for young children as learning a first language; they learn spontaneously from the language of everyday life. However, when only English is spoken in school, a child who does not already speak the language is at a great disadvantage. He is being asked to learn to read and write and to learn arithmetic, history, science, etc., in a language that he does not yet comprehend. This is a recipe for failure, even for a gifted student.

Because a non-English-speaking student can arrive in this country at any time during the school year, he will be placed in a class where the other students already know one another and the school routines, and have participated in a certain amount of group learning. The new arrival must adjust to the students, the routines and the curriculum all at the same time. Typically, he is placed in the class appropriate for his age, yet he may have had very little previous schooling. He may come from a place where educational opportunities were limited or his schooling was repeatedly interrupted. Some adult students may be functionally illiterate in their native languages as well as English; they need to acquire basic language skills. Even those who have previously studied English have been exposed to very different courses of instruction.

English is a difficult language to learn. There are many inconsistencies in spelling and pronunciation, and many exceptions to almost every rule. Because the difficulties are well known, many readers encounter an additional barrier of anxiety and fear, and when they are fearful, they are more likely to meet with failure.

For foreign speakers, understanding spoken English is equally difficult. How would a Navajo, Greek or Spanish speaker interpret the sentence *"He hit the nail on the head?"* Idiomatic expressions are usually interpreted literally— and immediately lose all meaning. Words that have several meanings or that sound the same are likely to confuse the foreign speaker, who may select the inappropriate one and lose the sense of the conversation. For example: *"The king reigned (rained?) for twenty years."*

Some English words and phrases, when pronounced with a foreign accent, sound quite different and seem to mean something different, which can be confusing to the listener and embarrassing to the speaker.

For example, the words on the left may sound like those on the right:

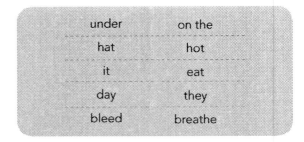

under	on the
hat	hot
it	eat
day	they
bleed	breathe

In English words, a single letter may represent several sounds. The letter *o* is pronounced differently in the words *Tom, hole* and *of*, as is the combination *ea* in the words *beans, bear* and *heart*.

Many foreign languages omit personal pronouns or use them in simplified form. English pronouns, particularly *he, she, his* and *her*, are therefore difficult for many beginners to learn correctly.

Be familiar with the obstacles your student must overcome in learning English, and show your confidence in him. With your help, he can and will learn.

Part II

Chapter 9: Guidelines for Teaching ESL

Self-Esteem

A student's self-esteem, and therefore his openness to learning, will be strengthened by his knowledge of and pride in his native culture. Look for biographies of heroes of his culture as well as descriptions of great historical events; your student will enjoy these, take pride in them, and maintain his interest in learning. Your neighborhood librarian will help you locate the materials you need.

As for all learners, instruction for the ESL student must focus on materials that will interest a student his age and motivate him to learn the skills that he needs. Keep in mind that there is no one method that is best for all students. Find the best way for your student.

Learning English: Speaking and Listening, Reading and Writing

Simple but real conversations should be encouraged from the first day. The meaning of what you say or read to your student should always be clear; make sure that he understands the material before having him repeat, read or practice. The best way to convey the meaning of a difficult subject is to relate it to the actual experiences of the student. Encourage him to speak about himself, his home, his community, his interests and his wishes and desires. As his speaking skills develop, he will be better prepared for reading, writing and participating in the total learning program.

You must speak and read to the student at a speed that allows him to follow what you are saying and to remember what he has heard throughout the listening period. In this way, he will be able to grasp the total meaning. Conversation and reading to the student about subjects of interest to him will help build listening skills.

Good pronunciation is learned most easily by imitation. Natural conversation provides the oral practice of new words, phrases and sentences by allowing the student to repeat what he has heard. If the student has difficulty imitating, or speaks with a heavy accent, remember that your goal is that he speak understandably, not perfectly. If you can understand him, his speech is adequate. Always try to limit the number of corrections; you want the student to feel successful. Praise him when you can understand him, and whenever he has overcome an obstacle.

Sometimes a student will have special difficulty with a particular sound: he may say *sheep* for *ship* or *pin* for *pen*. If his accent or dialect makes it difficult to understand him, you may want to give him practice in saying these sounds correctly. Always practice the sounds as part of words, not by themselves; sounds in isolation will lose all meaning for the student.

Children under twelve will learn to speak without an accent more easily than will older learners. If you are teaching a young child, be confident that having conversations with you as well as playing with other children his age and even watching television will contribute to his learning to speak English well. Remember that in criticizing a child's accent or dialect, you will be criticizing his family and his community. When correcting the student, concentrate only on a specific sound used in different words.

Vocabulary: Function and Content Words

Vocabulary may be divided into content words and function words. Concrete content words are those we can see, touch and illustrate. They are names of things (nouns), action words (verbs), and words that describe nouns and verbs (adjectives and adverbs).

Function words are the connecting words that have little concrete meaning in themselves, but which make it possible to understand the total meaning of statements. These are prepositions, auxiliaries and conjunctions, such as *and, on, to, the, by, for, but, how*.

Content words are easier to teach and easier to learn when they are very concrete and related to the experience of the learner. Consider this sentence:

The <u>big brown truck drove</u> over the <u>new bridge</u>.

The content words are underlined. Because they are concrete, they are easy to illustrate and to explain to the learner.

In the sentence *John is very <u>loyal</u> and <u>honest</u>*, the (underlined) content words are abstract, and therefore, more difficult to visualize and to explain.

When you teach the non-English-speaking student, begin with content words representing things and actions that are easy to illustrate and to visualize, and that the student can associate with hearing, touch or smell. As you set these words into sentences in your conversations with the student, you are also presenting function words to him naturally. Although these words are more difficult to learn, they will become part of his vocabulary as he learns to converse with you. You may introduce content words by:

- pointing to objects in the room and naming them.

- naming objects pictured in magazines and books.

- preparing a grab bag of objects; have the student reach in, take them out one at a time and name them.

Reserve the abstract words until your student is able to converse with you in a relaxed way and has acquired a useful vocabulary of concrete words.

Be careful not to use contractions at the beginning. Say *I do not* rather than *I don't*; *I will not* rather than *I won't*. Contractions are difficult to learn at the beginning and tend to confuse the student. Once he is able to converse comfortably, he will be able to learn the contractions more easily. On page 86 are common phrases, expressions and categories that are helpful to the student who is learning to speak English.

Some Spanish speakers may drop the final s sounds in their native language, and the habit can be carried over into English. Students from other countries may have similar habits. Look upon this as part of an old mannerism rather than an error. Eventually your student will learn to retain the final s.

Remember that all of us understand much more of the language than we use. Your student will also recognize and understand more words than he is able to incorporate into his own speaking vocabulary.

Teach Anyone To Read: The No-Nonsense Guide

Comparing Words in Different Languages

The English language has a debt to many languages; basically Anglo-Saxon in origin, English has borrowed a wealth of words from Latin, Spanish, Greek, Native American and other languages, both ancient and living, from all over the world. It has many words in common with some of the languages spoken by your students. In addition, other languages have borrowed English words and incorporated them. For example, in French, we now find the word *rosbif* (roast beef).

On the following pages are comparisons of similar words in Spanish and English.* You can make similar comparisons of words in English and the language of any of your students.

*Adapted from "Vocabulary Guide of Cognate Words in Spanish and English," by Stanley Krippner, Maimonides Hospital of Brooklyn, New York.

Some words are spelled the same in English and Spanish, most often ending in *or*, *al* and *able*.

- decimal
- continental
- formidable
- general
- conductor
- considerable

Some words in Spanish can be changed to English by dropping the final *a*, *e* or *o*.

Spanish	English
apparente	apparent
cosmetico	cosmetic
forma	form
idiota	idiot
inconveniente	inconvenient

Words ending in *cion* in Spanish end in *tion* in English.

Spanish	English
donacion	donation
graduacion	graduation
mocion	motion
ocupacion	occupation

Some words in Spanish can be changed to English by doubling the first, second or last consonant.

Spanish	English
ilegal	illegal
mocasin	moccasin
mision	mission

5

Some words ending in a or o in Spanish end in e in English.

Spanish	English
delicado	delicate
globo	globe
impulso	impulse
medicina	medicine

6

Some words ending in -ia or -io in Spanish end in -y in English.

Spanish	English
diario	diary
infancia	infancy
monopolio	monopoly
geometria	geometry
memoria	memory

7

Some words spelled with c or t in Spanish are spelled with ch or th in English.

Spanish	English
eter	ether
catedral	cathedral
coral	choral
autor	author
caracter	character

8

Some words ending in cia or cio in Spanish end in -ce in English.

Spanish	English
palacio	palace
servicio	service
distancia	distance
presencia	presence
silencio	silence

Teach Anyone To Read: The No-Nonsense Guide

9

Some words ending in *fia* or *phia* in Spanish end in *phy* in English.

Spanish	English
bibliographia	bibliography
caligrafia	calligraphy
topografia	topography

Some words that end in *dad* in Spanish end in *ty* in English.

Spanish	English
variedad	variety
vitalidad	vitality
capacidad	capacity
velocidad	velocity
oportunidad	opportunity
claridad	clarity

10

NOTES

Teach Anyone To Read: The No-Nonsense Guide

Chapter 11: Useful Word Lists for ESL Instruction

Colloquial and Idiomatic Speech

Idiomatic expressions can be a very confusing part of learning any new language, as can sound-alike words and many compound words. On the following pages are lists of words and phrases that require special attention when instructing ESL students. Also listed are sentences and categories that they will find helpful to learn. No doubt you will think of many more examples.

Selected Idioms*

A-1	As a matter of fact	Ax to grind
Of age	As yet	Back number
All at once	At fault	Back on his feet
All ears	At first blush	Back out
All in	At least	Back up
All in all	At your fingertips	Bad blood
All right	At my wits' end	Bag and baggage
Apple of my eye	At the top	Burst into tears

Compound Words

farfetched	sourpuss	screwball	hothead
shorthand	beeline	breakdown	dropout
daylight	bandwagon	holdover	makeup
browbeat	highbrow	handout	blackout
headshrinker	afternoon	windbag	greenhorn
aboveboard	skyscraper	checkup	breakfast
firsthand	halfhearted	layoff	workout
shorthand	lowbrow	bottleneck	

See pages 172 ff. for additional compound words, figurative language, idioms and other words that are difficult for many people to understand, especially students for whom English is a foreign language.

---

*For additional idioms, see *Word Play, A Dictionary of Idioms,* by Lillie Pope (Book Lab, 2001).

Words That Sound Alike: Homophones

to	too	two	tutu
but	butt	close	clothes
sink	zinc	sole	soul
hear	here	weather	whether
sell	cell	wear	where
hole	whole	do	dew
sail	sale	mail	male
umpire	empire	gorilla	guerilla
seam	seem	son	sun
bury	berry	fair	fare
which	witch	stair	stare
scene	seen	there	their
meat	meet	sew	so
minor	miner	knew	new
cent	scent	roll	role
holy	wholly	see	sea
by	buy	bin	been
lessen	lesson	one	won
reel	real	desert	dessert
die	dye	plain	plane
right	write	affect	effect
be	bee	waste	waist
rode	road	ball	bawl
no	know		

⭐ Common Phrases and Expressions That Are Helpful for ESL

My name is ____.

I live at ____.

I go to school at ____.

I am in the ___ grade.

My teacher is ____.

My telephone number is ____.

My e-mail address is ____.

I am thirsty (hungry.)

I do not understand.

Please speak more slowly.

Please repeat.

I do not feel well.

My mother is sick.

I was late because ____.

I was absent because ____.

I need to go to the bathroom.

Can we play this game?

Can we read this?

How are you?

I am fine, thank you.

Where is ____?

How much is ____?

I am very sorry.

Good morning (afternoon, evening).

I want to eat lunch.

I want a drink of water.

I would like a glass of milk.

The line is busy.

There is no answer.

Who is speaking?

This is ____ talking.

You have the wrong number.

I wish to speak to ____.

I am cold (hot.)

Yes.

No.

Please.

Hello.

Good-bye.

Thank you.

Excuse me.

I like cake (bread, milk, fruit, egg, etc.).

Where is the toilet (bathroom)?

It is there.

It is here.

What is your name?

What is your address?

Where do you live?

Which bus (train) goes to ____?

Did you eat breakfast (lunch, dinner)?

Are you hungry?

What time is it?

Common Phrases (cont.)

What time do you have?

It is ____ o'clock.

What time does the bus leave?

It is early (late, very early, very late).

Yesterday (today, tomorrow).

Last night.

This afternoon.

This morning.

What day is this?

Today is _____.

Today is a beautiful day.

It is hot (cold, cloudy, raining, sunny, windy).

What will the weather be tomorrow?

The sun is shining today.

Can I find it on the internet?

☆ **Categories**

Clothes

Parts of the body

Colors

Days of the week

Furniture

Months of the year

Coins

Food

Family relationships

People (girl, boy, man, woman, child)

Numbers

When your student has learned enough English words to be able to hold simple conversations with you, he is ready to begin learning to read. If he already knows how to read his native language, he will learn to read English quickly. Find out what he knows so that you can use this as a foundation for what he needs to learn. Be patient, be confident and keep in mind that he has special obstacles to overcome. Provide him with the opportunity for success and pride in his achievement.

NOPQRSTUV
WXYZABCDE
FGHIJKLMN
OPQRSTUVW
XYZABCDEF
GHIJKLMNO
PQRSTUVWX
YZABCDEFG
HIJKLMNOPQ
RSTUVWXYZ

Part III

Teaching Basics

Teach Anyone To Read: The No-Nonsense Guide

Part III

Chapter 12: Teaching Reading

General Guidelines for All Students

The ability to listen and to speak develops naturally during a child's early years. Reading and writing, as we know, must almost always be taught. A holistic philosophy of teaching holds that the most effective way of teaching those skills is to structure the program around engaging the student in discussions of subjects of importance and interest to him, providing a variety of materials with which the student can learn successfully and encouraging pleasure in learning. This includes:

- reading to the student.
- reading by the student.
- frequent conversations and discussions.
- a great deal of writing.
- a multi-sensory approach.
- the use of varied educational approaches in the learning situation.

While your challenge is to help students succeed, it is almost as important for them to take pleasure in practicing the skills they have learned. Helping a student learn to enjoy books, newspapers and conversation is one of the great achievements in teaching.

Methods and Techniques

Frequently you will read or hear about a breakthrough method of teaching reading that leads to inevitable success and renders all other approaches out-of-date. Actually, many methods will work with most students, but not with all. This chapter offers brief descriptions of several leading methods. But first, there is a critical distinction between the two types of reading instruction: developmental and remedial.

Developmental reading instruction is for beginning readers, including young children and a very small group of adults who have never been exposed to any kind of reading instruction.

Remedial reading instruction is meant for students of any age who have been exposed to instruction but have failed to learn what was expected of them. Generally, such students have learned something, but learned it unevenly.

> Would you believe that forty-three commonly used English words account for half of the words actually spoken in English, and that nine account for fully a quarter of all spoken words? The Big Nine are *and, be, have, it, of, the, to, will* and *you.* These nine words account for one-quarter of the words in written English as well.
>
> *Atlantic Monthly* 3/88

With this group, it is especially important to determine what the student has learned and what he has not learned—in other words, to use diagnostic teaching. Once having established where your student has succeeded and where he needs help, you can explore how your student learns. Then you can teach him to read.

Sight Words, or the Whole Language Approach

This method emphasizes the learning of whole words by recognizing the appearance of the whole word. Each word must be memorized independently.

More than 200 words in the English language are used so frequently that it is important for the beginning reader to recognize them automatically; knowing these Sight Words makes it possible to read and understand meaningful material early. See page 111 for a list of these words. (Languages using ideographic writing, such as Chinese, must be learned exclusively by this method.) A young child who watches TV learns many of these words from commercials by this method.

When this approach is used in school, the intention is to give the child early satisfaction in getting meaning from the material he reads. Picture and context clues are helpful in recognizing words taught by the sight-word method. When the student has learned enough words, it is important that he acquire the ability to sound out unknown words and thus expand his reading vocabulary. It is obviously impossible, and unnecessary, to commit the whole language to memory by sight.

Sounding Out Unfamiliar Words: Phonics, or Decoding, Approach

The decoding approach emphasizes the sounding out of words. By learning and applying the rules for sounding out individual letters and combinations of letters in a word, the student is able to sound out the whole word. For example, the student can sound out the word *late* correctly if he has already learned that the final *e* is silent and that this gives the *a* a long vowel sound. Since English is not a completely phonetic language, there are many exceptions to each rule. Nevertheless, the rules are followed often enough for the knowledge of phonics to be essential. The Phonics and the Linguistic Methods are both examples of the decoding approach to beginning reading instruction: both teach the student to associate sounds with letter symbols in order to "crack the code." To minimize failure and to remediate those who have failed, it is wise to teach decoding skills in simple, orderly steps.

Experience, or Write-Your-Own-Book, Technique

This is an invaluable method for capturing the interest of a young child or of an older student who has been difficult to reach; the crucial benefits are that the instructor gets to know which subjects are most meaningful to the student and the student works with material that interests him. The student dictates a story, or a series of thoughts, to the instructor; the instructor, or the student if he is able, writes it down or types it. The story becomes the student's reader; he learns the words, reads the story and expands on it in successive lessons.

The Multi-Sensory Approach

To capture and maintain the student's interest in the learning experience, it is important to involve all of his senses and to have him learn by doing. For example, the student may hear a recipe for baking brownies, write down the recipe and read it, mix and bake the brownies, inhale their fragrance and taste them. The student will learn from the lesson and enjoy it as well.

The Individualized Approach

Recognizing that individuals differ in skill, aptitude and interest, many educators attempt to match the instruction to the individual, using the method or combination of methods they deem most suitable for each student. Some students have superior visual memories, others have good auditory memories and still others learn best by being active or by touching.

To be most effective, the reading teacher should be open to using something from all the methods described above: phonics, for learning by hearing; Sight Words, for learning by seeing; written practice and forming letters with one's hand, for learning by action; and cut-out letters and different textures (clay, velvet, sand, etc.), for learning by touch.

This approach also relies on the presence of an extensive library of good literature in the classroom from which the student selects books to read at every opportunity.

Which Method Should You Use?

If your school, your supervisor or your agency uses one method, or one set of books and directs you to use that one, that is the method you should use.

If your supervisor does not recommend a particular method, or if a supervisor is unavailable, study the teaching materials provided in your program. These materials will often determine the method you use.

If no specific method is prescribed, the Individualized Approach can be easily adapted for most students. Use your ingenuity, selecting from the materials provided on the basis of the student's interests, attitude and ability. Generally, the emphasis will be on informal materials created by the teacher or materials that are easily obtained and inexpensive.

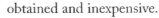

94

NOTES

Teach Anyone To Read: The No-Nonsense Guide

Chapter 13: Literacy

Comprehension

As mentioned earlier, the ability to read requires the simultaneous use of many skills. On its most basic level, reading requires the ability to understand the meanings of printed or written symbols. At the same time, it is necessary to understand the meaning of each word and the sequence of words.

Thus, in order to read the sentence *Tom is very tall*, the reader must know:

- that English is read from left to right.
- how to sound out the consonants *t*, *m* and *v*.
- how to sound out the short vowels *o* and *e*.
- how to blend consecutive sounds into a smooth-sounding word, such as "*v/e/r/y*" into the word *very*.
- how to comprehend the meaning of the word *is*.
- that *Tom* is a proper name.
- the meaning of the word *tall*.

After the reader becomes proficient at decoding and understanding the literal meaning of the printed word, his goal expands to include recognizing and comprehending the deeper meaning of what he is reading. The student who has gained confidence in his new skills will eventually feel comfortable enough with the written material to read alternate meanings into it, analyze it and ask critical questions about the writer's intentions. At an advanced level, therefore, reading sharpens the thinking involved in many of the thought processes used to meet and cope with the demands of life. In order to guide your student on his path toward literacy, it is necessary to determine his specific skill levels. Let's start with some definitions of the terminology often used by educators.

Many people are labeled *illiterate*; however, the term is broad and often not accurately defined or understood. A person who is *completely illiterate* cannot read at all, or can read only a few words. The term *functionally illiterate* is sometimes applied to a person who reads at or below the fourth-grade level. A functionally illiterate adult may read well enough to comprehend signs, simple instructions or perhaps an illustrated tabloid newspaper, but not to decipher instructions for assembling or repairing equipment, decode contracts or leases or read newspapers or books. His reading ability is inadequate for jobs that require more than the simplest reading.

For the purposes of instruction, reading is often described in terms of grade level. Grade levels are assigned according to the school grade in which a student is expected to master the given material as well as according to the relative difficulty of that material. The number of words in a sentence, the number of syllables in the words, and the content are all contributing factors. For example, students in the third grade are expected to read at the third-grade level; a level of 3.2 is the student's level of mastery in the second month of the third grade. As the student is able to read more involved material and can absorb concepts of greater complexity, he attains a higher grade level.

The tests used to determine reading grade level are not necessarily accurate indicators of a student's true reading ability. The score may be influenced by the design of the test, the way he was tested, as well as by any of several external factors. (To better understand reading levels and the skills they reflect, ask your supervisor for a copy of a written reading test and take it yourself.) In general, however, establishing a student's reading grade level is helpful as a rough guide to use in refining your assessment of a student's reading difficulties. Here is a description of each grade level for the purposes of reading instruction. To help you appreciate the significance of a given reading level, we will describe what is generally expected in each grade, though many students function ahead of and behind the fixed levels.

Levels of Literacy

Emergent/Budding Reader: Readiness for Formal Reading Instruction

Usually Age 5 (Kindergarten)

The student can differentiate shapes; knows some of the letters; knows that one reads from left to right; and is familiar with books, knows some of them very well and, ideally, has pleasant associations with them. In recent years, formal instruction has been given in some kindergarten classes.

Emergent/Budding Reader

Usually Age 6 (First Grade)

The first-grade student learns to recognize some words at sight; learns to read easy books using the Sight Word, or Whole Language, approach; learns to associate sounds with the consonants and the short vowels; and acquires the ability to blend consecutive sounds smoothly to form words.

Second-Grade Level

Usually Age 7

The student continues to read simple books in the classroom and learn more ways to analyze words. She learns the consonant blends.

Third-Grade Level

Usually Age 8

The student's reading becomes smooth and fluent. Reading is no longer a goal in itself but is now a tool for learning in other areas.

Fourth- to Twelfth-Grade Level

Usually Ages 9 to 17

At every grade level, the student improves her reading and study skills. Her vocabulary—the words she comprehends and speaks as well as those she reads—continues to expand. At this level it is hoped that she enjoys reading.

Chapter 14: Estimating Your Student's Reading Level

Reading Levels

Use a series of graded readers. (A graded reader is a school text marked with the grade level for which it is intended.) Select a sample of reading material near the end of each book in the series; each sample should be about 100 words long. Have your student read to you, beginning with the book you are fairly confident she can read easily. If she misses no more than five words, have her read a sample in the next (more difficult) reader. Continue in this way until she makes six or more errors in one 100-word sample.

The highest grade level at which she missed five or fewer words indicates her *Instructional Reading Level;* this is the challenging level at which the student should be taught. The grade level at which she read without assistance and missed only one or two words indicates her *Independent Reading Level.* The grade level at which she missed six or more words marks her *Frustration Level.*

Some of your students will be unable to read any of the books in the series fluently. Some students in higher grades, or even older adults, may be able to read only a few letters of the alphabet and one or two words. Such students read at the pre-primer level.

Instructional Reading Level: At this level, the student is able to:

- read 95 percent of the words.
- understand 75 percent of the ideas contained in the passage.

Independent Reading Level: Usually one grade level below the Instructional Reading Level, this is the highest level at which a person can comfortably read without assistance. The student is able to:

- read 99 percent of the words.
- understand 90 percent or more of main ideas.
- read smoothly and conversationally, and interpret the punctuation correctly.

Frustration Level

This is the level at which the student finds the material too difficult. It is usually one grade level above the Instructional Reading Level. Here, the student:

- reads fewer than 90 percent of the words.
- understands less than 50 percent of the material.
- struggles with many words.
- is unable to read smoothly because of the massive effort needed to decode the words.
- is frustrated!

Aural Comprehension Level

When this grade-level material is read to her, the student:

- understands at least 75 percent of the words and ideas.
- discusses it using vocabulary at the same level as the material and contributing her own knowledge and experience.

How to Evaluate Comprehension

As a reading instructor, you must know how to differentiate between the student's general level of comprehension and her level of reading comprehension. Students in reading programs can usually understand spoken language at a far higher level than they can read. The distinction between these two levels of comprehension is important.

To evaluate reading comprehension, have the student read a story silently from each book in the series. Have her answer questions about the main ideas, the vocabulary and the details. The book in which she answers correctly 75 percent of the questions is at her Instructional Level. If there is a discrepancy between this level and her reading level, the instruction should begin at the lower level.

When a student's comprehension skill is greater than her reading skill (frequently the case with older students who are learning to read), discussions should be more advanced than her reading level. To evaluate the student's general level of comprehension, read stories aloud from higher-level books, and discuss the main ideas, the vocabulary and the details. Once you have determined her comprehension level, it is important to converse with her at that level daily about matters of interest and importance to her. In that way, you will support and advance her "thinking" skills as well as her reading skills.

When the Student Reads at the Third-Grade Level or Below

Through formal or informal evaluation procedures (see pages 101–104), find the answers to the following questions about your student:

1. **Is she able to read a selection?**

2. **Does she understand what she reads?**

   Does she remember the details of what she has read?

   Does she understand the main idea?

   Does she see relationships: cause and effect, and similarities and differences?

   Does she understand the sequence and organization of what she has read?

   Is she able to draw inferences and conclusions from the reading matter?

3. **Is she confused or inconsistent in following the printed line from left to right?**

   If so, does she know left from right?

4. **How many basic sight words does she know?**

   Which words are unfamiliar to her?

5. **What skills has she acquired in sounding out unknown words?**

   Does she know the sounds of the consonants?

   Does she know the short vowel sounds?

   Does she know the long vowel sounds?

   Can she blend letter sounds fluently to form words?

   Can she read the consonant blends?

   Does she know the consonant combinations, or digraphs such as *ch, sh, th, wh*?

   Can she recognize vowel combinations, such as *oa, ai, ou, ow*?

   Can she read vowels followed by *r (ar, er, ir,* or *ur)*?

6. **Is her inability to sound out words the result of her not having learned to discriminate between similar sounds when she hears them, such as *lap* and *lack*, or *some* and *sun*?**

Don't forget that students with foreign accents or dialects may have difficulty pronouncing sounds as you do; this is not important. It is important that they learn to hear the differences in sounds, as an aid in word recognition.

The answers to these questions will pinpoint your specific goals in teaching the student. An inventory that is useful for evaluating some of the items just listed, particularly those relating to phonetic skills, is on page 109. Keep in mind that your day-to-day observations of your student's abilities are also important and relevant to your evaluation. In addition to the specific reading skills to be observed, the student's problems, interests, behavior patterns, work habits, patterns of speech, evidence of stammering or stuttering, motor coordination and general skills must be taken into account. The more you understand these factors, the more effective your planning will be. Your observations will also be important to your supervisor or a specialist, if it becomes necessary to consult one.

Remember to chat with the student about her interests, vocational goals, recreation and school experiences. In this way, you will be better informed about your student's problems and needs and their relation to your program.

When the Student Reads at the Fourth-Grade Level or Above

By the time she has learned to read at the fourth-grade level, a student has usually learned to sound out unknown words, and therefore does not need much help in that area. If you discover some weakness or confusion in sounding out words, turn to page 130 for suggestions for dealing with this problem. Otherwise, a discussion of materials and strategies used to teach the student at this reading level begins on page 161.

Concentrate on increasing vocabulary. Teach her how to analyze new words by breaking them down into syllables and by learning base words, prefixes and suffixes. Introduce study skills, and have her practice them so that she learns to use reading more efficiently as a tool in learning other subjects. Focus on comprehension skills, and introduce the student to works of literature, so that she learns to love good books.

Before moving on to your student's evaluation, keep in mind that the word "test" has unpleasant connotations for many students, implying that they might fail. It is not really an accurate term for the process. "Evaluation" or "inventory," on the other hand, denotes a focus on the student's strengths, weaknesses and interests for the purpose of improvement, rather than to pass judgment on her competence.

Part III

Chapter 15: Pope Inventory of Basic Reading Skills

How to Find Your Student's Reading Level

This inventory will assist you in evaluating your student's strengths and weaknesses in beginning reading skills.*

Dedicate a few pages in a notebook to keeping a record of how your student responds to these questions. In addition to defining her strengths and weaknesses, her answers will establish a place from which her progress can be measured.

> If your student makes five errors in any group of questions that follow, move on to the next group; if she makes the same or similar errors in three groups, stop the evaluation. This and any other inventory in reading instruction must be administered with great sensitivity, to minimize feelings of failure, frustration and pressure on the part of the student.

1. Does she know left from right?

Ask these questions only if your student is under 12 years of age. Circle the responses in the appropriate column at the right.

Point to your right eye.	Correct	Hesitant	Incorrect
Point to your left ear.	Correct	Hesitant	Incorrect
Which is your right hand?	Correct	Hesitant	Incorrect
Point to your right ear.	Correct	Hesitant	Incorrect
Point to your left eye.	Correct	Hesitant	Incorrect
Which is your left hand?	Correct	Hesitant	Incorrect

* Pope Inventory of Basic Reading Skills, by Lillie Pope, Book-Lab, Inc., Brooklyn, New York.

2. How much Sight Vocabulary does she have?

Common Sight Words

The following words are encountered so frequently in reading that it will be helpful for your student to learn them quickly, even before she masters sounding out words. Many of the words on this list will already be familiar.

Many Sight Words present a particular challenge to students with reading problems. Some words are easily reversible *(on, no)*; others have subtle differences *(came, come)*. The boldface words are those most frequently confused. In order to learn to recognize them easily, students require a great deal of practice.*

Present the words listed below, each word on an individual card, and ask the student to look at every card, dividing them into two piles as she goes along: "Friends" and "Strangers." Ask her to read the words she knows. She should be able to read them with ease and without hesitation. Count those she reads correctly.

Her Sight Vocabulary is _____ words.

*Excerpted from the Pope-Dinola Word Bank, by L. Pope and A. Dinola, New Directions Press

Sight Words

a	am	but	her	**that**	small	work	**want**	white	between
I	you	use	**saw**	only	**away**	after	your	thing	together
in	she	let	way	this	many	**then**	find	peace	thought
is	one	the	**how**	kind	**came**	**them**	**what**	under	because
on	can	eat	his	first	right	down	start	**never**	another
it	did	old	it's	**they**	home	love	found	those	through
as	and	may	call	gave	take	long	going	**every**	
to	**was**	far	into	read	around	goes	thank	little	
or	had	get	still	each	than	give	light	which	
so	own	any	said	send	some	keep	black	**where**	
up	two	big	tell	best	been	over	write	would	
by	him	**now**	just	here	**when**	same	great	funny	
be	see	say	left	**must**	with	know	think	school	
at	new	our	look	both	show	**went**	about	woman	
if	**for**	too	**most**	city	**from**	play	**there**	please	
an	not	man	stop	full	have	soon	today	should	
no	are	off	will	walk	more	good	**their**	before	
we	has	try	why	year	back	open	other	poison	
us	out	buy	like	does	time	exit	these	better	
me	all	**run**	girl	don't	keep	**come**	could	danger	
go	put	ask	very	made	were	done	bring	people	
do	who	boy	ever	**even**	seem	draw	house	enough	
my	its	day	well	help	much	make	again	**always**	

Teach Anyone To Read: The No-Nonsense Guide

3. Can she hear the initial consonants?

Auditory Recognition of Initial Consonants

Before reading from the word list below, say to the student, "I will say a word to you. Write down the sound that you hear at the beginning of the word."

If the student fails to write ten sounds correctly, ask her to repeat the sounds to you. This will tell you whether she hears the sounds correctly, even though she is not yet able to write the letters associated with them.

(d) daily	(g) gown	(s) sober	(m) marry	(f) fish	(h) happy
(j) jam	(r) rabbit	(b) barber	(p) pile	(l) lazy	(n) naughty
(t) top	(k) kit	(v) vat	(z) zip	(c) cat	

4. Can she hear the final consonants?

Auditory Recognition of Final Consonants

Before reading from the word list below, say, "I will say a word to you Write the sound that you hear at the end of the word." If the student fails to write ten of the sounds correctly, ask her to repeat the sounds to you. This exercise will tell you whether she hears the sounds correctly, even though she is not yet able to write the letters associated with them.

bird (d)	sedan (n)	topaz (z)	miss (s)	robe (b)	boil (l)
half (f)	dialogue (g)	fight (t)	lock (c,k)	stream (m)	soup (p)

5. Can she blend separate sounds to form a word?

Blending Sounds

Before reading the following sounds, say, "I will say two sounds. You tell me what word they make."

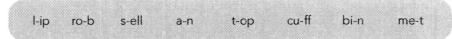

l-ip   ro-b   s-ell   a-n   t-op   cu-ff   bi-n   me-t

6. Can she recognize the consonants and associate the correct sounds with them?

Visual Recognition of Consonants

Present each consonant on a separate cards and ask the student to say the sound for each letter presented to her.

When you present the letters c and g, remember that each has two sounds. If the student gives one of the proper sounds, tell her that is correct, and ask if she also knows another sound for that letter.

If the student finds it difficult to give the sound for a letter, ask if she can think of a word that starts with the same sound.

7. Can she read the short vowel sounds in words?

Visual Recognition of Short Vowels

Present the following word pairs on separate cards and ask your student to read each word.

fed fad	lag lug	rot rut	lit lot
fin fen	rip rap	lip lop	gam gum

8. Can she read the short and long vowels?

Reading Knowledge of Vowels

Present the following words on separate cards and ask the student to read each word.

mat	din	fun	late	robe
let	rob	mate	dine	fume

9. Does she reverse letters?

Present the following words on separate cards and ask the student to read each word.

pal	no	raw	tar	pot	keep
tops	meat	never	even	saw	tan
won	rats	nap	read	lap	was

10. Can she hear the consonant combinations?

Auditory Recognition of Consonant Blends and Digraphs

Before reading the following words, say, "I will say a word to you. Write down the sound you hear at the beginning of the word. It will be composed of two or more letters."

(sm) smoke	(sl) sloop	(spr) spring	(ch) choose
(st) stand	(spl) splendid	(gl) glue	(cr, kr) crank
(sn) snore	(gr) grow	(sk) skill	(bl) black
(dr) drive	(str) stripe	(br) brass	(tr) trip
(pr) practice	(sh) shape	(sk) skate	(wh) wheel
(fr) frank	(pl) plaster	(fl) flower	(sp) sparrow
(th) thank	(cl,kl) clay	(sw) swing	

If the student fails to write ten sounds correctly, ask her to repeat the sounds to you. This will tell you whether she hears the sounds correctly, even though she is not yet able to write the letters associated with them.

11. Can she recognize the consonant combinations?

Visual Recognition of Consonant Blends and Digraphs

Present the following letter combinations on separate cards and ask the student to say a word that begins with the same sound.

sh	sm	gl	pr	fl	spl	bl
ch	dr	sk	sl	cr	spr	sp
th	gr	tr	str	scr	br	
wh	pl	st	cl	sn	sw	

12. Can she read the vowel combinations?

Reading Knowledge of Vowel Combinations Including Vowels Followed by "r"

Present the following words on separate cards and ask the student to read each word as best she can.

coal	firm	bawl	free	avoid	spray
laid	lie	maul	meant	joy	brew
took	morn	low	leak	nook	
burn	lout	harm	term	howl	

13. Can she separate compound words into their component parts?

Reading Knowledge of Compound Words

Present the followings words on separate cards and ask your student to read each word as best she can. After each word, ask which two words were used to make the one she just read.

breakfast	cowboy	anytime	grownup	afternoon
showplace	grapefruit	grandchild	senseless	barefoot

14. Can she read words with prefixes and suffixes attached to the root word?

Reading Knowledge of Prefixes and Suffixes

Present the following words on separate cards and ask your student to read each word as best she can. After each word, ask what it means. After four words have been read and defined correctly, ask the student how she analyzed each word.

export	unbuckle	preview	disown	rerun
meaner	meanest	meanness	hopeful	tension
lively	attendance	porous	seasonal	rotation

15. Can she separate words into syllables to facilitate reading them?

Syllabication

A. When hearing them (Aural)

Before reading the following words, say, "I will read a word to you. Tell me how many syllables are in each word."

mansion	direction	like	generous	dictionary
one	twenty	friendship	many	amendment

B. When seeing them (Visual)

Present the following words on separate cards and ask your student to read them, even if she has never seen them before, and count the syllables in each one.

wonderful	gentleman	knowledge	grandiose	delight
introduce	vocabulary	Manchester	fantastic	adrenaline

NOPQRSTUV
WXYZABCDE
FGHIJKLMN
OPQRSTUVW
XYZABCDEF
GHIJKLMNO
PQRSTUVWX
YZABCDEFG
HIJKLMNOPQ
RSTUVWXYZ

Part IV
Guidelines for Teaching at Individual Levels

Teach Anyone To Read: The No-Nonsense Guide

Part IV

Review: Thinking and Communication Skills

- Establish what your student knows and what he must learn:

- Set simple goals, so that he quickly achieves some success.

- Focus your teaching on his interests.

- Teach something he has indicated a desire to learn.

- Provide variety in every lesson.

- Frequently remind your student of what he has achieved.

Help your student develop and apply his thinking and communication skills so that he can evaluate and then articulate his understanding of what he reads. Following are some of the complex steps involved in understanding what we read:

- differentiating between fact and opinion

- differentiating between fantasy and reality

- noting the order of events

- grouping things that are similar, and categorizing them

- putting information in logical order

- recognizing the main idea

- recognizing the lesser details, and judging their relative importance

- questioning information and logic if there is insufficient supporting evidence

- problem solving

- perceiving similarities and differences between this and other information

- interpreting the information and events described

- seeing the relationship between cause and effect

- predicting or anticipating what might happen next

- inferring a reasonable conclusion from the information

- figuring out the author's purpose

- relating what one reads, hears or sees to the information one has already absorbed

- remembering

- comparing and contrasting

Encourage careful thinking in all conversation and discussion with your students relating to current events, television and media events, reading matter or any subject at hand. By asking him questions about his reading and experiences similar to the examples listed below, you can help your student develop comprehension skills.

- Who, when, what, where, why?
- What happened first?
- What do you think will happen next?
- How do you think things will work out?
- Did you like the main character in the story? Why or why not?
- Were you surprised by anything? Why?
- Would you have changed the ending? How?
- How are these two (stories, characters, problems) similar? How do they differ?
- Why did this (event) happen? What caused it?
- Why do you think the author wrote this?
- Do you have any idea from this story what kind of person the author is?
- Can you separate the author's opinion from the facts?

Understanding Abstract Concepts, Idioms, Metaphors, Colloquial Expressions and Slang

The words *table* and *chair* are understandable because they can be seen and touched, but words that are abstract, such as *loyalty* and *integrity*, are more difficult. The meaning of these words must be demonstrated through providing many examples of their proper use.

Expressions such as "My eyes popped" or "When I heard this, my heart dropped," can be confusing to ESL students, and often to young children. Be certain that the student understands each of these as they are read or heard; they must be defined, with many examples of their use.

Part IV

Third Grade Level and Below

Achieving Your Goals

If your student reads at third grade level or below your goals are to:

- build and maintain his interest in learning to read.
- associate pleasure and success with the printed word.
- teach him to read automatically from left to right.
- teach him a basic vocabulary that he can recognize at sight.
- teach him how to sound out unfamiliar words.
- teach him to analyze the structure of words as an aid in reading.
- help increase his vocabulary.
- help increase his comprehension of reading matter.

Read all the steps below and use the ones you think will work best for you and your student.

☆ Step 1: Recognizing Words at Sight

Sight words may be taught by means of the experience approach as well as through the use of word lists. To help the student build a stock of words that he recognizes at sight, the vocabulary must be coordinated around his interests.

Write-Your-Own Book

The experience approach is helpful in instruction at every level. Its main technique is the Write-Your-Own Book, which is essentially a book created by the student for his own reading instruction. The teacher assists in writing down the material as it has been expressed by the student. Because the Write-Your-Own Book is based on the interests and experiences of the individual student, it can motivate, as well as focus the student to work toward his goals.

Your student will already know some words from earlier studies, advertising or daily life. Start your student off with a vocabulary list of these words, words he already recognizes at sight. Steadily add to this list as you focus on the words he uses to describe his life or thoughts. Review this list often. This is how you will help him lengthen his list of sight words. These words will make it possible for him to read and write more meaningful material while he is acquiring greater skills.

It is helpful to set aside a writing area into which students may withdraw to think about, and then write about their fears, thoughts, experiences, hopes, ambitions and observations. As the student expresses himself in writing, his reading skills are reinforced. Do not criticize spelling errors; your goal at this time is to encourage written expression. If the spelling is criticized, the student may resist writing.

How to Prepare a "WRITE-YOUR-OWN" Book

1. Have your student or students describe an interesting or dramatic experience. Let the students dictate the story to you so that you can type it into a computer or write it down in their own words. The story can be about anything.

2. Use the student's natural and colloquial expressions. Editing and re-writing should be done rarely, carefully and never without the knowledge and agreement of the student. Many students tend to dictate run-on sentences or endless numbers of "and"-connected sentences. Here your guidance is valuable: keep the sentences short. Try to vary the sentence structure. Substitute periods for the "ands" without disturbing the flow of dictation. If words are repeated too often, discuss alternatives with your student.

NOTE: When the student dictates a contraction (can't, don't), write the word as he dictates it. After he has reread the story, it will be helpful to point out to him that this is the short form of two words that ordinarily look a little bit different:

When written out, "can't" is "cannot," "don't" is "do not."

3. Whether the manuscript is printed out or handwritten, the lettering should be clear, bold, black, attractive, neat and easy to read. If handwritten, it will be important to make a photocopy of the completed manuscript. Be sure to save the document if it has been stored on a computer. Several copies will come in handy for later use.

4. To make a cover for the book, clip the story into a folder. This will be the first of a number of chapters to be inserted into this folder. Have the student print a title and his name on the cover. If your student is a schoolchild, or if you feel he has an interest in illustration, encourage him to create pictures for the stories and the cover. Collage is a wonderful method for students of all ages and levels of artistic confidence to introduce visual images into their stories. When possible, photographs of the student can be used to heighten the impact of the book.

5. Have the student read the story back to you. If he hesitates over some words tell him what they are, and then print each one on a separate card. Let the student practice reading the unfamiliar words from the card as well as the book.

6. Another way for your student to use his story as a basis for practice involves taking the extra copy and cutting it up into words, phrases or sentences. Let him read the "cut-ups," arrange them into new sequences and read them back in the new order.

7. At the next lesson, review the new words with him. Have him reread the story. Discuss it with him. Then, ask him to dictate a new chapter, following the same process as before.

Your student's "WRITE-YOUR-OWN" Book can take the form of:

- a scrapbook, illustrated with pictures that he draws or cuts out of magazines.

- a book or play that he and you write as part of your dramatic play together.

- a newsletter or newspaper for the tutoring or reading center.

- a "how-to" book about something he likes to do, such as "How to Build a Scooter" or a cookbook.

When making a "How To" book with your student, consider working on one of the projects described by the student, if the facilities allow for such work as baking or building. Research for the book may involve looking at library manuals, following their instructions, making shopping lists for the necessary materials and equipment and actually shopping.

Dramatic results are possible with this technique, particularly when a teacher uncovers a subject of great interest to the student. At such times, the student may even learn to read long and difficult words, like "coagulate" and "extricate," before he learns the short, commonly used words such as "this," "then" and "these".

Teach Anyone To Read: The No-Nonsense Guide

Word Lists

In addition to the words derived from the "Write-Your-Own Book," it is essential to teach as sight words the common words that make up at least 50% of all reading matter. These words are listed on page 111. At each lesson, a few minutes should be spent learning the words that are still unfamiliar to the student. To provide variety in practicing these and any other words or sounds the student is learning, several helpful devices are described in pages 161–170.

Any device or game that will provide interest and variety in practice can be used. Always try to appeal to as many of the senses as possible: pronounce the word; have the student write it, trace it or feel its shape after it is cut out of materials of different textures, such as sandpaper or velvet; have the student say it or act it out.

Encourage the beginner to look for words and letters everywhere: to hunt around on the back of tin cans and cereal cartons to find letters and words that he recognizes and knows; to look at street signs, computer screens and advertisements for numbers that he knows, for the letters in his name and for words that he can recognize or sound out as he learns phonic skills; and to look at television commercials, magazines, newspapers and even billboards. Every new recognition should bring with it a feeling of victory.

Abbreviations as Sight Words

Abbreviations are encountered frequently and may be difficult for the student to decipher. They should be taught to him as sight words. Here are some of the more common and important abbreviations.

P.S.	Public School	p.	page
H.S.	High School	etc.	et cetera, and so on
M.S.	Middle School	pp.	pages
&	and	4th	fourth
Ave.	avenue	c/o	care of
St.	street	A.M.	morning
Blvd.	boulevard	P.M.	afternoon
Mr.	mister	P.S.	postscript
Mrs.	title of a married woman	S.O.S.	cry for help
Ms.	miss	lb.	pound
M.D.	doctor of medicine	Dr.	doctor
D.D.S.	doctor of dental surgery	vs.	versus
oz.	ounce	C.O.D.	cash on delivery
ff.	following	mph	miles per hour

Reminder: Teach the abbreviations for the months of the year and the states of the union.

☆ Step 2: Sounding Out Unfamiliar Words

Make a list of the sounds your student already knows, but do not teach them again. On the Sound-Out Sheets located in Part III you will find word lists that will help you determine what new sounds you need to work on with your student.

Try to teach sounding out in the following order:

1. the consonants whose sounds do not usually vary

2. the short vowels

3. the remaining single consonant sounds

4. the long vowel sounds

5. the remaining special sounds.

The student should learn a key word that uses each sound learned.

1. The Consonants Whose Sounds Do Not Usually Vary:

b, d, f, h, j, k, l, m, n, p, r, s, t, v, w, z

How to Teach a New Sound

a. Be sure that your student recognizes the sound you are teaching, and can distinguish it from other sounds. To teach the consonant *b*, first have your student listen to the sound of *b* words: *bill, but, boy*. Then have him select the words that do not begin with the same sound from another group of words: *ball, bat, bounce, cat, bay*. Have him tell you words that start with the sound of *b*.

b. Now he is ready to associate the sound with its letter and with its key words (in this case, *ball*). Write a list of words beginning with *b*. Pronounce each word as you write it. Have him pronounce it, too. Have the student point out in what way the words sound the same and look the same: they all start with the same sound, and the letter that represents that sound at the beginning of each word is *b*. Once more, have him tell you other words that begin with this sound, and list them. Have him write the letter, together with the key word and its illustration, in his notebook.

Teach Anyone To Read: The No-Nonsense Guide

Avoid giving the sound of any consonant in isolation. If the student learns the sound of the letter *b* as *buh*, it will be difficult for him to blend sounds. It is best to demonstrate the sound of *b* by saying the key word for that sound, *ball*.

c. Involve all of the student's senses in associating the letter with its sound. Have him write it in the air, on the board, on paper, in sand and with clay, or shape it with pipe cleaners, whatever works for that student, while at the same time saying words that begin with that sound.

d. Now the student is ready to sound out words using the new sound. It is important to practice recognizing and pronouncing the new sound in words as quickly as possible. Present the new letter in words of one syllable, associating it with sounds that he already knows, so that he may blend them together to form a word that he can recognize: *bat*.

e. As soon as he has learned to read his new sound in words, the student is ready to practice reading that sound in sentences. Prepare sentences that use that sound frequently: *Bob is at the bat but Bill begs Ben to be a bit better.*

Reminder: Some students have difficulty learning new sounds; they need a great deal of practice and repetition; and their instructors need a great deal of patience.

2. The Short Vowels*

After several of the consistent consonants with their key words have been taught, the student is ready to learn the short vowels.

Start by teaching the short a sound, together with its key word, apple. Show the student how this sound, placed between the sounds of two of the consonants he knows, makes a word: he can now sound out the words h-a-t and b-a-n. It is important to help him blend the sounds smoothly, to hold one sound until next one is begun, and to feel satisfaction at the recognition of a word that he can now read for the first time.

He should practice blending, using his known consonants and the short a, as in:

| tap | sad | man | dab | pan |

*Additional word lists are on pages 172–220.

After the a, introduce the short *i* sound. It can be taught in the same way, using

pin   sip   mid   fit   hip

Review the a and the *i* sounds by presenting a list of mixed words;

man him lit fan pin nip ran sad bit had

Teach the sound of short *u*.

jut   bun   rub   mud   pup

Review the three short vowels together.

jut lip rat ran sat bun mud fun sip

Following this, teach the short *e*. Many students find it difficult to differentiate between the short *i* and the short *e* sounds.

net   fed   hen   set   leg

Review the four short vowels.

man pen lit pin ran net jut him sad

Teach the sound of the short *o*.

hop   dot   bob   not   rot

Review all the short vowel sounds

kit   not   set   ran   sun   pat   rob   hen   tin   bun   man   sod   mill

3. The Remaining Single Consonant Sounds

The student is now ready to learn the remaining consonant sounds, with the key words, and to use them in blending with the vowels.

c as in *cat*   *c* as in *cent*   *g* as in *gallon*   *g* as in *gin*

The sound of *y* as in *yet* and of *q* and *x* may be taught later on or when the need arises.

4. The Long Vowel Sounds

Because the sounds of the long vowels are the same as the names of the vowels, the student will have little difficulty learning the sounds. He must, however, learn the following instances of when to use the long vowel sounds.

The *e* at the end of a word is always silent, giving the preceding vowel the long sound.

fine   rave   pure   lone   sake   mete

In words where one vowel follows another, the first vowel sound is pronounced by name and the second vowel is silent, as in the following double vowel words.

deem   meat   rain   oak   loan

*Lists of words using these combinations are on pages 190–197.

5. The Remaining Special Sounds

Consonant Combinations*

Use each of the following consonant combinations in a number of key words. It will be important to teach these combinations carefully because it is actually very difficult to hear and repeat these combined sounds clearly

sl	pr	cr	fr	br	tw	pl	cl
bl	fl	gl	sc	sk	sm	sn	sw
gr	tr	dr	sp	st	spl	spr	str

Additional Consonant Sounds

The student must learn the additional consonant sounds formed by *sh*, *ch*, *th*, and *wh*. Even though each of these is a pair of letters, the pair represents one sound, and is treated as one sound. The consonant sounds of *ph*, *ng* and *gh*, that do not occur as frequently, may be taught as the need arises during reading instruction.

sh	shop	fish	shell	shape	cash
ch	chin	chip	chop	chat	chill
th	thing	thick	thin	think	thank
wh	whiff	which	when	wheel	while

Review the special consonant sounds.

shape	play	chip	clock	thing	skin	spot
blow	flame	whip	glass	grow	pray	stiff

Additional Vowel Sounds

oo as in *soon*	*au* as in *maul*	*ar* as in *bar*	*ir* as in *stir*
ow as in *slow*	*ay* as in *day*	*or* as in *for*	*ur* as in *burn*
oo as in *book*	*ow* as in *owl*	*er* as in *her*	
oi as in *oil*	*y* as in *my*		

As the need arises, special vowel sounds should be taught to the student. At that time, systematic practice in these sounds should be given.

☆ Step 3: Analyzing the Parts of Words

By learning how to break words down into their smaller parts, your student also learns to build new words into his reading and speaking vocabulary. Fluent readers learn to recognize frequently occurring prefixes, suffixes and roots, and to combine the parts of compound words.

Compound Words*

Sometimes a student who can read single words is confused when these words are put together to form compound words. He must be helped to see compound words as two words put together. Have him practice reading the parts, and then the whole words:

news	paper	newspaper
can	not	cannot
farm	house	farmhouse
cow	boy	cowboy
grand	child	grandchild

---

*See page 204 for a helpful list of compound words.

Base, or Root, Words and Common Word Endings

To help identify base, or root, words, list a number of sets of words that have common roots. Have the student find the base word of each of the following

asked	asking	asks	
helping	helpful	helper	
running	runs	runner	
sleeping	sleeps	sleepy	
farmed	farming	farmer	farms

Make up exercises in which the student fills in the appropriate base word and ending. Use the base word *sing*.

John is a good ____.   Jane ___ well.   Tom is ___ a hymn.

Prefixes

Prefixes must be recognized as units, separated visually from the rest of the word. It is important for the reader to learn the meaning of the prefix, so that he may know how it alters the meaning of the base word.

When the prefix or suffix is attached to a word whose meaning one already understands, it will be easy to understand the total word (the base word, with a prefix or suffix attached to it.)

It is very important to have a dictionary nearby. As your student reads a passage, make a list of the words he does not understand. Look up in the dictionary every word that is not clear and encourage your student to do the same even when he is on his own. Have him read the paragraph after he has understood all the words. He will appreciate the difference in his ability to comprehend the material.

Note how the prefixes placed before the words in each of the following columns change the meaning of the words.

re	fill	tell	read	write	print
dis	like	appear	approve	courage	agree
un	even	true	fit	lucky	happy

Following are a number of common prefixes, together with their usual meanings, and with examples of words in which they are used.

in meaning *not*, as in:
informal   incorrect
inhuman   invisible
insincere

in also meaning *into* or *inside*, as in:
income
indoor
inland

**dis meaning *not* or
the opposite of, as in:**
dislike
distrust
disarm
disagree
disorder

en meaning *in, into, make*, as in:
enable   enlighten
enforce   enjoy
enclose   enlarge

ex meaning *out, out of*, as in:
expel
exit
exhaust

pre meaning *before*, as in:
prehistoric
preview
prepaid

re meaning *again*, as in:
replace   replant
repeat   reclaim
recall   review
recharge   renew

un meaning *not*, as in:
unwise   uneasy
unsound   unjust
untidy   uneven

Suffixes

Suffixes can be taught in the same way as prefixes. The common suffixes are *-ly, -er, -est, -tion, -ness, -ful, -less, -ous, -ious, -ent* and *-ment*. Note how the suffixes create new words when placed after the words in each of the following columns.

ful	wonder	care	help	thought
ly	quick	sweet	kind	slow
ment	enjoy	settle	improve	agree
less	sleep	pain	thought	help
est	tall	slow	fast	strong
er	tall	slow	fast	strong
ous	joy	poison	marvel	glory

-ful meaning **full**, as in: skillful   powerful   restful   frightful

-tion meaning **a condition, or the process of, or the product of doing what is described by the base word** as in:
attraction   collection   digestion   connection   exception

-ness meaning **the state of being bright, plain or whatever word it is attached to,** as in:
brightness   likeness   highness   plainness   thickness   readiness

-ment meaning **the product of doing the activity that is described by the base word,** as in: achievement   investment
atonement   placement

Dividing Words into Syllables

Your student does not need to know all the rules of syllabication, but he should have some understanding of how to reduce a long word to its simple elements so that he can read it more easily. He should know that every syllable has one vowel sound, and that each vowel sound identifies one syllable. With this information he can listen to a word, count the number of vowel sounds, and know the number of syllables. Since only vowel sounds count, silent vowels are to be ignored. Double vowels *(oo, ee)* have one vowel sound, as do special vowel combinations, such as *ou, ow, oi, oy, ay, au, aw.*

Recite unfamiliar long words to the student, and have the student count the syllables. After the student has learned to count the syllables in a word, he is ready to divide words into syllables. He is ready for the following simple rules:

1. When two consonants are between two vowels, the syllables are divided between the consonants.

Af—ter   les—son   bas—ket   num—ber

2. When a word has a vowel-consonant-vowel sequence, the consonant is usually part of the first syllable if the first vowel is short as in *pris—on* and *tax—i.* The consonant becomes part of the second syllable if the first vowel is long as in *e—vil, mu—sic,* and *sil—lent.*

3. When "le" is at the end of a word of more than one syllable, the last consonant joins the "le" to make the last syllable:

ta—ble   trem—ble   stum—ble   bu—gle   rat—tle   puz—zle

Teach Anyone To Read: The No-Nonsense Guide

☆ Step 4: Encouraging the Student to Read a Story

Both oral and silent reading are important. When the student reads aloud, you are able to hear hesitations and errors, and to help when he is stuck. However, he may be embarrassed to hear himself stumble, and therefore may be unable to concentrate on the meaning while he reads aloud.

When reading to himself the student can read more quickly and is less embarrassed. When he meets an unknown word that he cannot sound out, he can often figure out its meaning from the context.

Be sensitive to the type of reading that is best for your student. Sometimes it will be better to read aloud and sometimes it will be better to read silently. Help your student to feel good about doing both.

To minimize anxiety in the student who lacks confidence in reading, it may be helpful to do the following:

- Allow him to read the passage or story silently before reading it aloud.

- Take turns; you read one line or sentence, and he reads the next one.

- Have the student read the selection into a tape recorder and then listen to himself.

- If possible, dramatize the selection. Each of you can play parts portrayed in the selection.

- Discuss the selection with the student before he reads it. Discuss the place, the theme, what to look for or what to expect.

- Interrupt the reading as little as possible. Interruptions will interfere with concentration and he will not be able to remember what he is reading.

- Overlook insignificant errors that do not change the meaning of the selection: *house* for *home*, for example.

- If he has difficulty with a word, tell it to him (do not let him struggle, even if you are positive that he can figure it out).

- Some readers mumble to themselves as they read silently, or form the words with their lips. Do not discourage them from doing so. When they no longer need this crutch, they will drop it.

- After reading the selection, discuss it. What was it about? Does it make sense? What happened first? And then what? And then? Why? If the student has difficulty answering any one of your questions, offer help within a few seconds. Don't let him feel that he has failed.

 NOTE: The goal is to have your student enjoy the lesson and feel successful. Learning to read will be the result of positive experiences.

☆ Step 5: Developing Comprehension Skills

As mentioned earlier, even in the early stages of instruction, a student can often understand a great deal more than he is able to read. His spoken vocabulary, intellectual concepts, and life experiences are often ahead of his ability to decipher the written symbol. After he has mastered the mechanics of reading, the emphasis in instruction should shift to expanding his understanding of what he reads. From this point on, raising his reading level means enlarging his vocabulary and his ability to interpret increasingly difficult material.

The reading matter used should be meaningful, absorbing and useful so that it will engage and hold the student's interest and attention. If the content of the reading fails to involve him, he will drop instruction as soon as he has mastered the minimal skills necessary to achieve immediate specific goals, such as reading the subway signs, passing the driver's test or filling out a job application. This is why the materials selected must cater to the needs, interests and level of competence of each student.

Activities

Here are a number of suggestions on how you may teach comprehension and study skills below the fourth grade level. Comprehension, as well as vocabulary, is sharpened through the use of oral discussion. Aim at clarity of thought and observation on the part of the student as you conduct the first three activities:

 CAUTION: Do not assign written reports or compositions to student at this reading level. While the Write-Your-Own Book activity is a wonderful aid at this point, independently written reports and essays are probably too difficult and will discourage the student.

- Have discussions centering on current matters of interest to the student (housing, medical care, job-related problems, hobbies, games).

- Have discussions relating to the mass media that reach the student (the internet, a television documentary, a rented movie, a picture magazine article, a music video).

- Have discussions relating to visits, made with or without the instructor, in which the student is encouraged to discover new things, or sees new aspects of old things, (museums, factories, zoos and parks).

- Read material to the student that has been chosen by the student.

- Make lists of words in interesting categories to increase vocabulary. For example, compile a list of words for preparing meals (food, sugar, meat, stove, oven, temperature), for repairing automobiles (car, engine, carburetor, mile, mileage), or for using the computer (reboot, virus, instant message, email).

- Use the student's own slang or colloquial language to help increase his vocabulary. Make a dictionary translating his words into those in more common usage; do not discourage him from continuing to use his colloquial expressions, but instead assist in expanding his vocabulary based on these special words. These words may be unfamiliar to you but he will translate them for you. You will find your own vocabulary expanding as he takes pride in teaching you!

Specific Comprehension Skills:

Following are specific comprehension skills that should be developed. The reading materials used by the teacher for these activities should be chosen or created by the student. Particular attention should be given to the techniques that improve clarity of thinking.

A. Selecting the main idea:

Make up several titles for a story, discussion, TV or internet site.

Select the best of several titles.

Tell (or write at the student's level) a summary paragraph describing the story, discussion, or internet site, etc.

Select the most important sentence of the paragraph.

B. Organization of ideas:

Choose a story.

Tell what happened in chronological order.

Tell what happened in logical order.

Organize simple sentences in the correct order.

Organize simple paragraphs in the correct order.

Find the answers to the questions *who, what, when, where, why* and *how.*

C. Finding details:

Make a list of important questions

Find the answers to these questions.

Fill in details that have been omitted in a report or discussion of a book, program or trip.

D. Following directions:

Give your student directions that he must follow. Start simple and increase complexity over time. Directions may involve how to find a book in the room, or another room in the building, on how to travel to a special place, how to make something or how to use a specific website.

Have the student give you similar directions. Be sure the student's directions are complete and can be followed; if the directions are unclear, have him fill in the missing details.

E. Drawing inferences:

Anticipate what will happen next in a story, or in current events.

Draw conclusions from information given.

Interpret the meaning of a sentence or a paragraph.

You can use some of these materials for the activities described above:

Daily newspapers

News for You, New Readers Press, Syracuse, New York. This is a high inter-est-level, easy to read weekly for use with adult beginning readers. Information is available online at: <http://www.news-for-you.com/index_h.html>

Write-Your-Own Book dictated by student

News telecasts and radio news broadcasts

Picture, sports and hobby magazines

Catalogues: mail order, sports, etc.

Technical manuals

Cookbooks

Appropriate internet site

☆ Step 6: Encouraging Writing Skills

Use of the Write-Your-Own Book activity is vitally important at this time. As your student's skills develop, the book he writes will become more complex and therefore a more adequate reflection of how he really thinks and feels about the world. This will provide real proof to the student that his skills are improv-ing and his work paying off. The key in this activity is enjoyment and success.

Part IV

Fourth to Eighth Grade Levels

Achieving Your Goals

- Help expand his enjoyment and interest in reading.
- Teach comprehension and study skills.
- Help correct his weaknesses in sounding out words.
- Help break down the patterns that cause him to make common errors.
- Help increase his vocabulary.

 Your goals for your student are to:

Remember: the student's interest level is higher than his reading level. Make sure that the reading material you select for your lessons is interesting to and level appropriate for your student. Keep a record of your student's most common errors so that they can be addressed in the lessons you design.

As your student reads more and more on his own, use the dictionary to help him expand his vocabulary. Look words up together as they occur in conversation or in the reading matter. When used frequently the dictionary can become an important and friendly tool. Alphabetize magazines, books on the shelf, whatever comes to hand. Find several definitions for the same word, analyze the meanings of words in which the prefixes are varied, the roots are changed, or the suffixes are changed. Emphasize comprehension in listening, in reading and in discussing.

Improving the comprehension and study skills of your student are overlapping activities. For instance, learning how to make a good outline is both an important skill in studying material and in taking it apart to analyze, and therefore, comprehend more completely. In fact, comprehension skills are the basis for any type of studying. Following is a recap of some of the activities useful in helping your student in the crucial areas.*

*Materials suggested on page 147 and those listed in the Helpful Publications section pages 239–257 can be used.

Step 7: Study and Comprehension Skills

Study skills may be developed through teaching your student how to:

- use the title page, table of contents, index.
- use the dictionary (as mentioned above).
- use the library.
- take notes on books and on class discussion.
- make an outline.

Comprehension skills can be improved by:

- making outlines of paragraphs, stories, programs and discussions.
- filling in simple outlines.
- describing the author's point of view.
- selecting the words and phrases that are editorial rather than reportage in news items.
- differentiating between subjective and objective statements.
- seeking evidence for information, when appropriate.
- identifying emotionally loaded words and phrases.
- reading and comparing several accounts of the same event or subject.

Step 8: The Writing Process

Spelling, writing and speaking skills develop as reading competence advances. Concentrate on vocabulary usage and improved organization of ideas. Overlook spelling errors; they may be relatively unimportant at this time. It is far better to say, "We'll work on spelling at some other time," to indicate to the student that, although the spelling is incorrect, the composition has merit. Remember that encouragement and sincere commendation for improvement and for work well done are the most effective incentives for continued progress.

Many students have so little confidence in knowing enough about any subject that they are totally resistant to expressing themselves in writing. They feel inadequate in spelling, in knowledge, and in the use of expressive language.

They need encouragement, support and assistance in realizing how much information they already have, and in learning how to get more information and how to organize that information so that they can write about it.

Beginning the composition or story:

A. Brainstorming

Choose a subject: pet dogs, medical costs, or a favorite teacher. Talk about it, listing every thought and every bit of information that comes out of the discussion as you go along.

B. Organizing

Help the student put the list in logical order. He can number the items without rewriting the list or, if he, or you, can type his list directly into a computer, it is extremely simple to re-order the list, in addition to numbering the points. Actually, this list has now become an outline for the written work he is about to do.

C. Writing

Following the outline the student can now write down his thoughts in narrative form.

D. Rewriting or Revising

Most students resist rereading and revising their written work, since they were reluctant to do it in the first place. More encouragement is necessary to help students analyze their own work and to look for the following:

- Did I say what I wanted to say?
- Have I been clear?
- Have I skipped over critical bits of information?
- Are there confusing passages?
- Have I left anything out?
- Does it make sense?
- Is there a better way to say a particular thing?

E. The Finishing Touches

The sensitive teacher will know which students are prepared to work on spelling, punctuation and legible handwriting. If you are able to maintain your student's drive to improve there will always be another day to work on handwriting.

Part IV

Ninth Grade Level and Above

Achieving Your Goals

Students who read at the ninth-grade level and have returned for remedial instruction are probably aware that, in order to qualify for technical occupations, a high school diploma or its equivalent (the high school equivalency certificate: see page 156 for information on GED exams) is necessary. Instruction for this group involves no new skills, but rather the further development of the skills taught earlier, such as increased vocabulary, heightened understanding of material read, greater critical evaluation, better study skills and greater appreciation and enjoyment of the printed word.

Step 9: Comprehension and Vocabulary Skills

After the mechanical aspects of reading have been mastered, comprehension skills are further developed through increased understanding and use of the printed page. Reading instruction now concentrates on helping the student understand and interpret what he reads. **Discuss and analyze reading material as much as possible!**

Keep vocabulary lists in a book or card file. Focus on words that are commonly used in the field in which the student hopes to work. **Keep using the dictionary!**

Step 10: Review Ways to Understand and Interpret Meaning

- Understand the literal and figurative meaning of words, sentences, selections.
- Understand the meaning of punctuation marks.
- Retell the story: what happened first, what happened next and what happened last.
- Get the main thought.
- Find the important details.
- Follow the instructions.
- Recognize relationships between ideas and characters.
- Make comparisons; see cause and effect.
- Predict outcomes and solutions.
- Draw conclusions.
- Make generalizations.

More Review and Tips to Support Critical Reading:

- Distinguish the significant from the trivial, relevant from irrelevant, fact from opinion.

- Evaluate material from the reader's perspective and from other criteria.

- Determine the writer's point of view.

- Read widely on controversial issues.

- Maintain an objective and inquiring point of view.

Step 11: Study Skills

Encourage the use of almanacs, atlases, encyclopedias and the computer. Students will need to use these reference works if they are asked to write an essay based on research. The student will know, perhaps with your help, what subjects will inspire him to do this research successfully. Almost everyone needs help in improving study skills.

Locating Information:

- using the title page and table of contents

- reading maps, diagrams

- using the glossary and index

- using the dictionary

- searching the internet

- using the encyclopedia and other reference materials

- understanding graphs and tables

- understanding the bibliography

- using the library catalog

Organizing Information

- alphabetizing
- listing
- classifying
- finding main ideas
- selecting important details
- skimming to find specific information
- summarizing
- outlining
- note-taking

Learning How to Study

- note-taking
- outlining
- anticipating questions and formulating answers
- reviewing

Committing Information to Memory

- rereading to aid in retention
- practicing, with intervals between each practice or study period
- continuing to practice until the response is automatic

Test-Taking

- overviewing the test
- judging how to allocate time for each question
- judging whether guessing is penalized on this particular test
- knowing when to skip a question and move on

Step 12: How to Prepare an Outline for a Report*

I. Introduction: An outline is an orderly arrangement of ideas and information. It helps to clarify ideas and to facilitate their recall by establishing relationships among them. The outline may be sketchy or detailed, depending on how it is to be used. Earlier a very basic outline was described. In this section you will find a more detailed and formal outline description and example.

II. Purpose

    A. To organize ideas and information for study and recall

    B. To organize ideas and information for the preparation of a written report or an oral presentation

III. Procedure

    A. Preparation

        1. In preparing an outline from material that the student hears, he must take notes and then treat those notes as though they were reading matter.

        2. To prepare an outline from material that he reads, the student should first skim the selection to get an overview of it, and then read the selection carefully, outlining it as he reads it.

        3. To prepare an outline for a written or oral presentation based on his own experiences, the student should list his thoughts, ideas and facts. He should then reorganize them into an outline.

        Sometimes it is helpful if the instructor asks leading questions to encourage the student in expressing his thoughts and ideas.

    B. Preliminary Thinking About Ideas and Details

        1. Identify the central theme.

        2. Identify the main ideas.

        3. Identify the details that support the main ideas.

            a. Sometimes they illustrate the main idea.

            b. Sometimes they explain the main idea.

            c. Sometimes they give reasons for or causes of the main idea.

            d. Sometimes they give chronological development of events of the main idea.

            e. Sometimes they give definitions of the main idea.

*See how the letters and numerals in this step are used.

4. Identify the relationships among the ideas.

C. Writing the Outline

1. Organize the facts and ideas according to:

   a. Sequence or

   b. Importance or

   c. Any relationship that you have selected

2. Insert supportive details (or facts) in the appropriate section, according to the organization you have selected.

3. Consolidate outline by:

   a. Combining ideas that are similar

   b. Discarding minor or inconsequential details

   c. Discarding irrelevant thoughts or data

   d. Avoiding repetition

4. Form of the Outline

   a. To indicate parallel and subordinate relationships easily, it is helpful to use a combination of letters and numerals in outlining.

      i. Roman Numerals—main thoughts or ideas

      ii. Capital letters—major details

      iii. Arabic Numerals—minor details

      iv. Lower Case Letters—subordinate details

      v. Lower Case Roman Numerals—minor subordinate details

   b. Subheadings may be added to clarify the meanings of headings.

   c. Each item is indented according to its importance. All listings of the same letter or numeral carry parallel or similar weight or value in terms of their relationships within the outline.

Materials

At this level, a great deal of reading matter is available and you can encourage your student to read many different types of material. Any reading that is successful and enjoyable helps develop reading power, even pulp magazines or tabloid newspapers. Allow ample time for discussion so that you and your student can discuss the different types of literature available to him.

General Educational Development (GED) Tests

Qualifying for the High School Equivalency Diploma

High school equivalency programs were launched in most states after World War II to enable veterans to earn high school diplomas. The high school equivalency diploma is the legal equivalent of a high school diploma for purposes of civil service requirements and is normally accepted as such by business concerns and the Armed Forces. Most colleges will accept the certificate for admission; inquiries should be made directly to the college of choice.

Information on how to file for high school equivalency tests is available from all local high schools, from the state or city education departments or from the following website http://www.lacnyc.org/hotline/GED/. While it is possible for your student to schedule the date and time of the test she will have to register and go to the testing center to take the exam.

All of your students reading at or above the ninth-grade level should be encouraged to prepare for this examination. It is a realistic goal, and one well worth achieving. With a diploma, the student can take advantage of education and training above the high school level, and command higher salaries.

The GED tests are designed to judge whether the student has the skills in literacy and math equal to the upper two-thirds of those currently graduating from high schools in the United States. About 800,000 adults take the GED test each year, and well over 500,000 of them are awarded high school equivalency diplomas. To learn more about the structure and demands of the test your student can visit the website mentioned earlier or do a search on the internet for local support and the most up-to-date information.

Grading the Examination

Each candidate's test score is determined by comparing results with those attained by a very large group of high school seniors. Consequently, candidates should not be discouraged by the difficulties of any of the examination items. Since almost two out of three candidates pass the examination, your students have a very good chance at succeeding.

The GED tests are designed to find out what the student knows, with less emphasis on how quickly the student can answer the questions. The student should aim at getting the highest score possible, but should not feel that he is competing with anyone else.

Nevertheless, there are time limits on the GED tests. The allowed time is always announced at the beginning of the test but, obviously, bringing a watch can help in keeping track of the time. There is usually enough time for most people to answer all the questions, but the student should learn to pace himself. Practice in preparing for the exam helps. If the student is afraid of tests, the best way to prepare and to combat fear is to take sample tests as frequently as possible.

Students can use the GED High School Equivalency Exam Books published by Barron's, Arco or Cambridge. These books contain descriptions of the exam and much practice material, and are easily obtained in major bookstores and online.

Excellent for the development of comprehension and study skills, these books also provide the practice in taking tests essential for your student at this point.

NOPQRSTUV
WXYZABCDE
FGHIJKLMN
OPQRSTUVW
XYZABCDEF
GHIJKLMNO
PQRSTUVWX
YZABCDEFG
HIJKLMNOPQ
RSTUVWXYZ

Part V

Support Materials

Part IV

20. Helpful Devices and Games
Lesson Plans
Three-by-five cards
Word Wheels
Tachistoscope
Television
Do-It-Yourself Games

21. Useful Word Lists
Illustrated Alphabet Key Words
Short Vowel Sounds
Long Vowel Sounds
Double Vowel Sounds
Double Vowel (Mixed) Sounds
Review of Short and Long Vowel Sounds
Consonant Sounds
Consonant Combinations
Consonant Combinations (Mixed)
More Consonant Combinations
Additional Vowel Sounds
Vowels Combined with the letter r
Words that Rhyme
Compound Words
Practice in Syllabication
Prefixes
Suffixes
Antonyms
Homonyms
Heteronyms
Selected Words with Several Meanings
Selected Idioms
Sample Comprehension Skills Exercises
Who? What? When? Where? Why? How?

Chapter 20: Helpful Devices and Games

Lesson Plans

Lesson plans are essential in classroom, small group and individual instruction. The principles of planning are similar in each situation.

The sample plan shown below is for working with a student who recognizes only a few words at sight and is learning how to sound out words. At present, this student can sound out a number of the consonant sounds and has just learned the sounds of the short *a* and *i*.

Sample Plan

Student: **Date:**

Teacher: **Lesson:**

Goals for Today	Activities	Comments	Next Lesson	Supervisors' Comments
1. Learn Sight Words.	Play Game: Go Fish	Went well.	Play this game again.	
2. Review sounds of short vowels <u>a</u> and <u>i</u>.	Use sound out sheets	Needs more drill on <u>i</u>. Knows <u>a</u>.	i	
3. Learn short vowel <u>u</u>.	Use sound out sheets	Is still hesitant.	u	
4. Develop comprehension.	Discuss TV show tutor and student saw last night	He needs encouragement to speak.	Assigned same show for next week. Remember to discuss it.	
5. Combine 1 and 4 above.	Student dictates a story for Write-Your-Own Book, based on discussion in 4.	Dictation went well. He cannot read many of the words.	Practice these words before attempting to reread story.	
6. Enjoyment of reading.	Read from newspaper a human interest story.	Picked the wrong story. Not interesting to the student.	Try something related to flying. Seems interested in that.	

Notice that the instructor has prepared for six different activities within the one session. The lesson includes:

- something old (review of short vowels a and i).

- something new (short vowel u).

- an opportunity for the student to discuss something interesting to him, thereby improving his use of spoken language.

- encouraging the student, as he dictates a story to the teacher, to use his own interests as a means of developing reading matter.

- an opportunity for the student to relax and derive pleasure from written material, when the teacher reads an interesting brief selection to him.

Clear and simple goals have been set for this lesson. Inevitably, some of the choices you make for a lesson will not work as well as you hoped. In the sample plan, the instructor has noted in columns 3 and 4 where some things went wrong. These notes are invaluable guides for planning the next lesson.

Three-by-Five Cards

These are the simplest, most flexible and most easily available of all teaching devices. They can be used:

- for words to be learned, each on a separate card.
- for word lists.
- for practice in reading a single sound, prefix or suffix.
- to encourage smoothness in reading.

fig. a

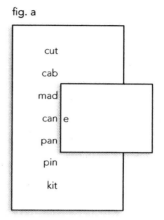

cut
cab
mad
can | e
pan
pin
kit

fig. a. List words on a card in which the short vowel sounds become long ones (with the addition of the final *e*). Near the edge of another small card, print an *e*; have your student place the second card so that the *e* is placed at the end of each of the printed words in turn. Ask him to read each word with and without the final *e*.

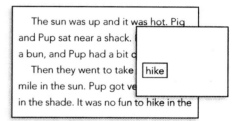

The sun was up and it was hot. Pig and Pup sat near a shack.
a bun, and Pup had a bit o
Then they went to take | hike |
mile in the sun. Pup got ve
in the shade. It was no fun to hike in the

fig. b

fig. b. Cut a rectangular slot in an unruled three-by-five card to form a window; place over the text to expose individual words or phrases. Determine the size of the window by the number of words you want to expose to the student's view at one time. Slide the card across the text as the student reads.

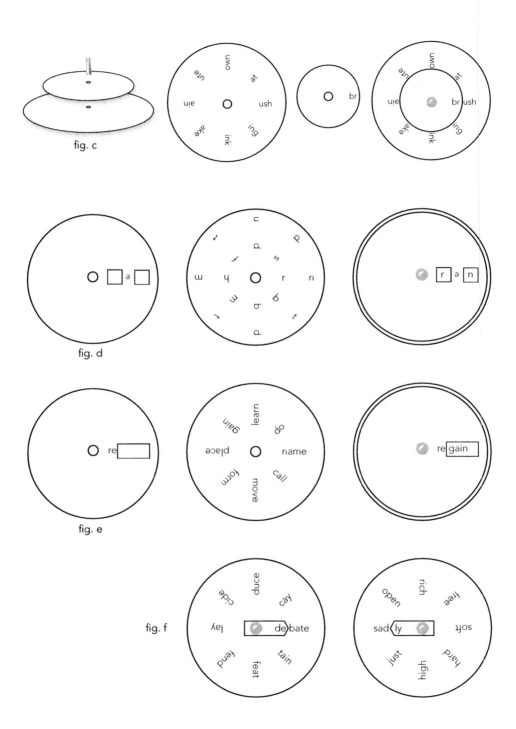

fig. c

fig. d

fig. e

fig. f

Word Wheels

Word wheels can be used to practice initial sounds, common word elements, final sounds, prefixes and suffixes. Here are several examples:

fig. c.   A simple wheel can be made of two circular pieces of cardboard, one considerably smaller than the other, with a small hole in the center of each. Place the smaller wheel on top and line up the holes; attach with a paper fastener. To practice forming words with an initial consonant sound, print the initial letters at the right edge of the smaller wheel and the appropriate word combinations around the larger wheel, as shown. When the top wheel is rotated, the two groups are matched up to form words.

fig. d.   To practice short vowels, cut two cardboard circles, one slightly smaller than the other, with a small hole in the centers. Cut two small windows in the smaller wheel and print a vowel between them. Print the appropriate consonants around the larger wheel, as shown, using the windows in the smaller wheel as a guide. Place the smaller wheel on top and line up the holes; attach with a paper fastener. When the top wheel is rotated, the letters match up to form words.

fig. e.   To practice prefixes, cut out the circles as above. Cut a word-long window on the smaller wheel and print the prefix next to it on the left, as shown. Print the appropriate base words around the larger wheel; attach. As the top wheel is rotated, the base words appear in the opening. For suffixes, print the letter to the right of the window.

fig. f.   For practice in adding prefixes or suffixes to words, print the appropriate word combinations around a cardboard wheel and attach cut-out pointers with a paper fastener, as shown.

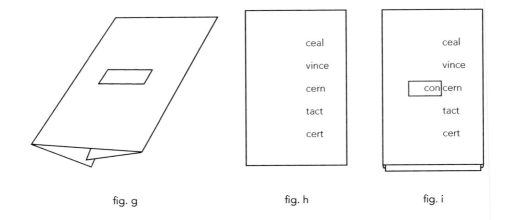

fig. g   fig. h   fig. i

Tachistoscope

This is another effective device for practicing word recognition. Cut a window in a strip of cardboard wide enough to fold into a four-inch-wide sleeve (fig. g). On another sheet of cardboard, slightly less than four inches wide, print the words that the student is learning (fig. h). The words should be at least three-quarters of an inch apart and positioned so that they will be exposed through the window one at a time as the inserted sheet is moved up and down in the sleeve (fig. i).

This device may be adapted for use with prefixes or suffixes. Print the prefix on the sleeve to the left of the window, or the suffix to the right. Print the base words on the sheet to be inserted in the sleeve and move it up and down, as above.

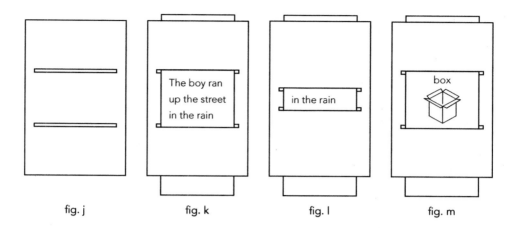

Television

In the center of a piece of stiff cardboard, cut two horizontal slits about two inches apart (fig. j). The slits should be one quarter of an inch from top to bottom and wide enough to permit a two-inch strip of paper to slide through. Adding-machine paper is especially suitable.

Clearly print short phrases on each line that tell a story. As the paper is pulled slowly through the slits, several lines at a time are exposed. For a young child, cut the slits further apart to make the opening larger, and illustrate the strip of paper (fig. k); you might let the student draw and color the illustration (fig. m).

This device can be adapted to help overcome word-by-word reading. Cut the slits no more than one inch apart so that only one line shows at a time (fig. l). This develops the ability to see as many words as possible at a single glance; in this practice, the phrases do not necessarily have to relate to one another.

Do-It-Yourself Games

Dominoes

Using word cards instead of tiles, the student matches words rather than dots. This game provides practice in reading and recognizing matching words, and helps the student distinguish between words that she may be substituting for one another, such as *on* and *no*.

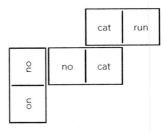

Making words

Have the student make as many words as she can out of the letters of large words, such as *government: go, me, govern, men, never, ever, even, ten, move, rent, grove, vent, over, trove, rove* and *more*.

Decoding

Write simple sentences or stories for the student, omitting the vowels. Have the student complete the sentences:

Wh_n w_nt_r c_m_s, c_n spr_ng b_ f_r b_h_nd?

Rhyming

Encourage the student to think of words that rhyme. Prepare a set of puzzles similar to the following:

Think of words that rhyme with *rode*, and complete these phrases

heavy _____   like a frog _____

The lawn was _____   the seamstress _____

Think of words that rhyme with *fate*, and complete these sentences:

Fish bite at _____.   The captain had a _____.

At lunch she _____.   Tardy means _____.

The fence had a _____ .

Teach Anyone To Read: The No-Nonsense Guide

Editing

Hand out or dictate a story and have the student rewrite it and make corrections. In some, prepare silly errors; in others, have the student practice punctuation. In this example, ask your student to add seven missing periods and seven capital letters.

Ellen ran to school she went to the class the teacher was in the room the boys and girls were in their seats a cat was in the room it had no seat the teacher took lunch money from everyone the cat had no lunch money.

Hidden words

Look for words among the letters at right, reading from left to right or from top to bottom. When the student finds a word, she will put an outline around it and write it at the side of the page. Can she find nine words?

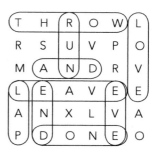

Buried sentence

Have the student make a sentence from the following letters, according to the instructions below.

s m l T a j z w	1. Start with *T*, down, right.	T _ _
a t o h e e l x	2. Start with *e*, right, down, left, down, right, right, up.	e _ _ _ _ _ _
c a n t h p e t	3. Start with *s*, down, right.	s _ _
a t b e e h a n	4. Start with *o*, down.	o _
	5. Start with *t*, right, down.	t _ _
	6. Start with *c*, right, up.	c _ _

[Answer: The elephant sat on the cat]

B	H	Q	O	W
K	C	U	J	P
M	G	F	D	R
I	Z	S	V	E
A	N	X	L	T

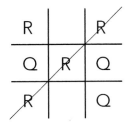

Bingo

Use five-column (down and across) bingo cards to practice letters, vowels, sight words, number facts, geography facts or any skill. Set up the bingo cards with letters, or words, numbers, names of cities, etc., and call out the name of the matching item. Instead of calling out the name of the item you can also display on a flash card. The player uses a marker (a piece of paper, a penny or a similar item) on the bingo square with the correct answer. The player who has five markers in a row in any direction wins.

Tic-tac-toe

Instead of using X and O, each player uses one word or letter that needs to be practiced, and the winner is the first one to complete a horizontal, vertical or diagonal row.

Anagrams, Charades, Ghost, Geography and Lotto

These games can also be easily adapted for reading instruction.

NOTES

Chapter 21: Useful Word Lists

Word Lists

The following word lists may be used in a number of ways to provide practice in sounding out words.

1. Present the lists to your student directly from this book. Show only one word at a time; cut a small window out of an index card and place it over the word.

2. Rewrite the words, as you need them, on index cards or sheets of cardboard. With a felt-tip pen, print each word large and clearly, leaving ample space between them.

3. If you write the words on separate cards, they may be used as flash cards. Be careful to present them to the student slowly at first.

4. Use word wheels and other devices to add variety and interest to the instruction (see pages 165–170).

5. Present the words in varied order, to be certain that the student recognizes each word.

6. Remember that the student needs a great deal of practice. If necessary, use more words.

Illustrated Alphabet Key Words

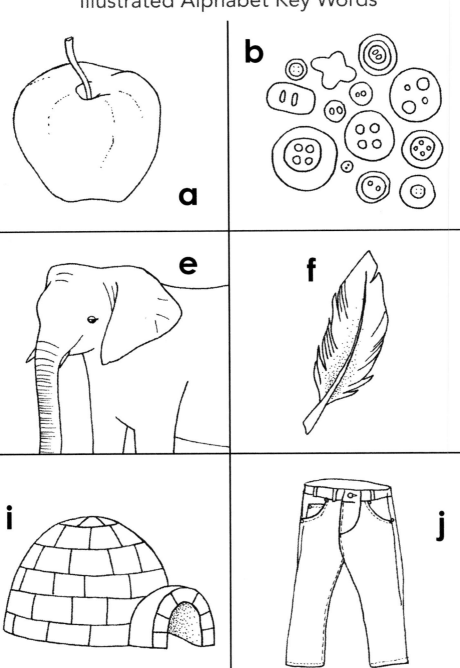

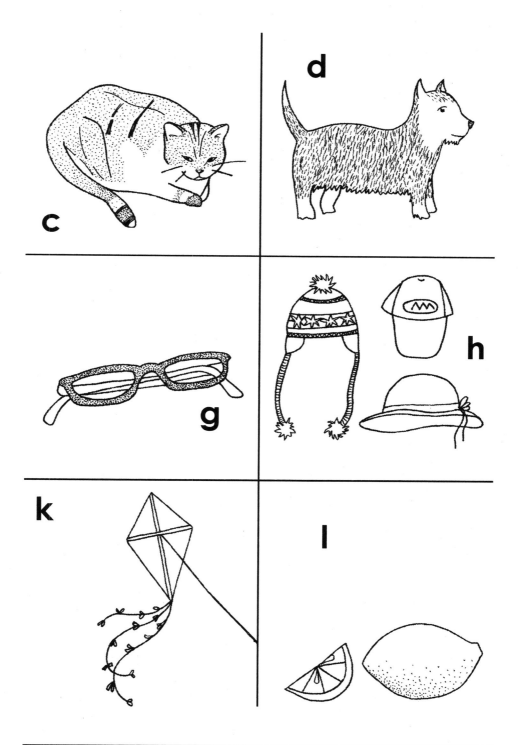

c

d

g

h

k

l

Teach Anyone To Read: The No-Nonsense Guide

m

n

qu

r

U

v

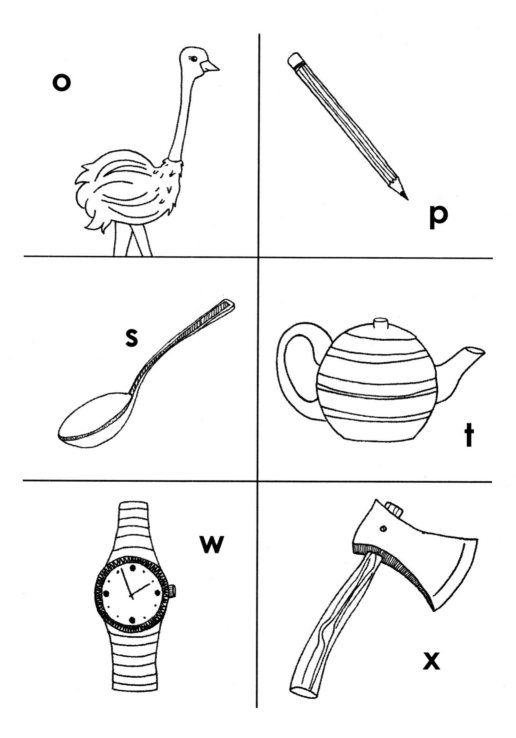

o

p

s

t

w

x

y

z

ch

sh

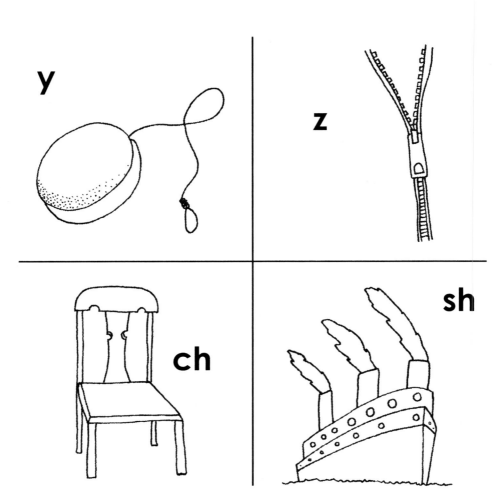

c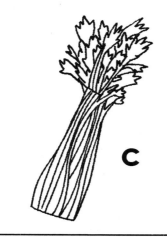

g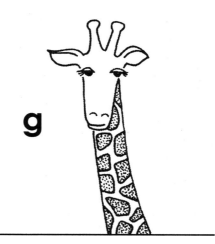

th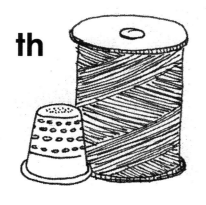

wh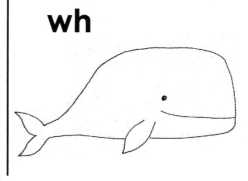

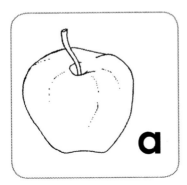

Short Vowel Sounds

Short *a*

sat	pan	can	an	rat	bad
am	map	sad	cab	mat	dad
had	lad	jab	ban	bat	ram
mad	bag	ham	ran	tan	pad
jam	fat	rag	dam	rap	tag
pat	sap	man	Sam	tap	sag
hat	fan	has	fad	pal	lap
add	at	gap			

Short *i*

sit	wit	win	hip	hill	rib
fit	dig	rip	his	him	did
hit	dip	fig	tin	sill	lid
fib	wig	dim	bill	rim	nip
tip	bid	bib	sip	in	big
sin	ill	fin	lip	miss	ill
bit	mill	jig			

Review of short *i* and short *a*

pan	dad	hid	pin	nap	rib
kit	pat	till	dim	ham	him
ran	bad	tap	had	fit	map
kill	hip	ran	rap	did	hit
bat	am	sin	bib	lip	fat
lid	fib	will	dam		

Short *u*

hub	but	us	hum	nut	fun
hut	rub	pup	dug	up	rug
sun	bud	mud	gum	nun	sup
bun	cub	tub	hub	rum	gun
jut	tug	bug	cud	bum	cut
run	bus	sub	rut	sum	hug

Review of short *a*, *i* and *u*

mud	fat	bad	rut	rib	bud	pan	kid	rub
man	kill	jut	bat	hat	sub	hid	till	map
bun	hut	ran	win	run	fib	sin	us	dim
cub	had	lug	rap	did	sup	bun	bib	hub
dam	tub	bus	ran					

Short *e*

red	men	mess	bed	fez	wed
net	pet	get	well	peg	less
den	jet	bet	Ben	Tess	vet
hen	wet	bell	let	fed	tell
led	keg	hem	pen	hep	set
ten	beg	Ned	fell	met	Meg
set	pep	Ted	sex	sell	leg

Review of short *a*, *i*, *u* and *e*

  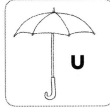 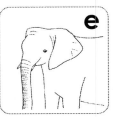

fell	ban	dug	less	kiss	den	tan	tell	hut
tub	hub	kid	tap	kill	ten	pet	dim	bun
sun	tag	had	bid	led	pen	mud	ill	rib
sit	let	but	fed	sub	mill	bat	Ben	

Short *o*

odd	hop	dot	lot	doll	rob
mob	hot	cob	hop	fog	top
pot	rot	job	not	cot	lop
nod	Tom	fob	pop	bob	sop
pod	sob	mop	cod	got	mod
rod	hod	sod	mom	tot	hog

Review of *all short vowels*

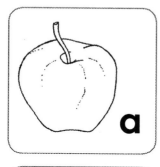

jam	get	will	rod	red	is	mob	sun	fin
add	wet	rot	jet	pot	run	mud	not	rob
sob	web	bud	bus	bad	dog	rat	bet	hot
jut	his	tap	hen	pup	lip	sin	well	man
pet	us	bed	tin	hut	bid	win	pan	web
bat	sap	pod	tub	hum	hip	cod	fan	mad
bun	dad	top	net	tip	bill			

Long Vowel Sounds

Rule: An *o* at the end of a word has a long sound.

no	so	go	yo-yo

Rule: When two vowels are together, name the first vowel and skip the second.

ee	deep	feel	peep	beet	deem	beef	weep
	deer	see	keel	heed	reel	fee	jeer
	need	meek	deep	feet	seed	weed	leek
	peel	reek	keep	reed	heel	week	keen
	lee	seen	feed	seem	wee	reef	bee

ay	say	bay	hay	way	may	nay	lay
	jay	day	ray	pay	play	stay	gay

ai	nail	pail	vain	bail	laid	hair	wait
	main	gait	bait	mail	maid	hail	pair
	plain	tail	raid	gain	paid	rail	jail
	fail	brain	pain	fair	sail	maim	wail
	rain	gain	wait	bait	lair	waif	aim

Double Vowel Sounds

ea	beat	neat	bead	tea	veal	peak	meal
	team	hear	bean	mean	beak	heal	wean
	meat	eat	ear	seal	read	leaf	beam
	deal	leak	leap	real	near	seam	fear

oa	oat	load	roam	foam	goad	oak	road
	goat	boat	road	coat	load	soap	oaf
	goal	foal	toad	loaf	moan	soak	oar
	coal	loan	hoax	moat	coax	roan	loam

ie	lie	pie	die	tie	lied	tried	cried

ue	hue	sue	rue	due	true	blue	clue

oe	doe	foe	Joe	Poe	toe	woe	

Double Vowel (Mixed) Sounds

nail	wait	sue	suit	seen	hue	wheel
meat	deal	aim	sea	soap	mail	load
oak	due	leaf	pie	neat	week	beat
need	deep	feet	eat	foe	hear	teem
team	chair	foam	roar	died	tie	leak

Silent *e* Rule: When you see a vowel-consonant-final e combination, name the first vowel and skip the e.

make	mine	ate	sale	file	pure	mile
zone	line	made	cure	mate	cute	lake
bode	lane	hole	male	rave	fine	kite
tube	cake	one	life	page	use	ripe
pole	bite	time	mole	cape	rise	gale
dote	dine	sole	same	bale	mice	cope
poke	pale	fuse	five	race	dome	bake
ride	mane	date	coke	vine	hike	dive
pine	cane	tune	tide	hate	rope	

Review of short and long vowel sounds

ripe	hop	fin	set	met	ran	goat
pad	hate	paid	bead	pine	not	tape
use	men	rob	neat	cub	rod	bed
bet	did	rode	can	pin	rid	tube
got	gape	mean	rip	lad	rain	died
pain	cane	dim	hat	mad	dime	tub
beat	pan	cute	rate	made	ate	cube
win	us	bait	robe	man	wine	meat
pet	rat	hope	laid	pane	road	cut

Consonant Sounds

c as in

cap	cod	can	cat
cub	cud	cuff	cot

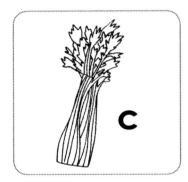

c as in

center	cell	civil	cement
cent	city	cellar	cereal

g as in

goat	go	gob	gal	gap
gut	got	gag	gum	girl

g as in

giraffe	gee	ginger	George
gender	gem	gin	gentle
general	giant		

qu as in

queen	quill	quite	quack
quarter	quit	quiz	quip
quick	question	quilt	

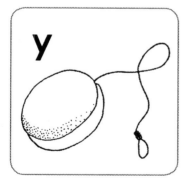

y as in

yo-yo	yet	yap	yak
yard	your	yellow	yam
yes	yell	year	you

Consonant Combinations

pl	play	plow	plan	plight	plea	plume	plank
	plain	plane	plate	plait	plant	plot	please
	plum	pluck	pleat	ply	plod		

cl	clock	claim	club	clang	clean	clip	clap
	clot	clean	clear	clash	clay	clam	Clark
	clerk	click	claw	clod	clump	clove	

bl	blue	blade	bless	bluff	blank	blink	black
	bleat	blond	bled	bleed	blood	blend	blare
	blunt	blurt	block	blind	blame	blaze	bleak
	blade						

fl	flee	flame	flag	flit	fleet	flea	flute
	fled	flour	flog	flick	flight	flare	fly
	flask	flirt	fling	flint	flesh	flash	

gl	glue	glass	glee	gleam	glow	gloom	glide
	glen	glean	glib	glum	glint	glimmer	glove
	glaze	glare	glad	glade			

sl	slide	slave	slid	slop	slap	sleep	slept
	slip	slay	sleet	sleigh	sled	sleeve	sloop
	slight	slinky	sloppy	slur	sling		

pr	print	proof	prove	pride	prune	preach	print
	prick	prism	prop	prize	price	press	prod
	prim	pram	pretty	proud	pray	praise	pry

cr	cram	cream	crib	crane	creep	crack	crush
	crop	crab	cry	crisp	crust	cramp	crag
	crash	craft	crazy	crease	creek	crime	crimp

fr	fresh	friend	frank	from	fray	free	frame
	frill	fright	fringe	frog	fry	frock	frond
	frisky	fret	freak	freeze	frail	France	frail
	froth						

br	bred	bread	braid	broke	brink	brand	brake
	break	bring	brought	brother	bride	brood	brush
	brand	breech	branch	brunch	brick	brown	broil
	brim						

gr	grand	gray	greet	groan	gruff	graze	grass
	green	grief	grape	greed	grill	gripe	grit
	grin	grime	grim	grab	grout	grog	ground

tr	true	tree	track	trick	train	truck	trunk
	tribe	trade	trail	tramp	trap	trash	tray
	treat	trip	trill	tripe	try	troop	trace

dr	drive	dress	dream	drill	drink	drank	drunk
	drab	drag	drake	drape	draw	drawn	dry
	drip	drop	droop	drool	drove	drive	drag

sp	spell	span	spit	spat	speck	spill	speak
	speech	spin	spine	spark	spank	space	spade
	spawn	spent	spun	spike	spool	spooky	spot

st	stand	still	stain	stone	stop	stay	stall
	stake	steak	stack	stag	stab	stage	stalk
	stem	start	stark	star	steam	stamp	stint

sc	scant	scat	scold	scowl	score	scoop	scan
	scale	scat	scum	scar	scour	scarf	scare
	scan	scalp	scout				

sk	skinny	skate	skin	skill	ski	sky	skit
	skid	skunk	sketch	skew	skim	skip	skirt
	skull						

sm	small	smell	smile	smart	smack	smite	smock
	smog	smut	smug	smash	smoke	smith	smooth
	smother	smear	smudge				

| **sw** | swim | sway | sweep | swell | sweet | swoon | swing |
| | swank | swear | sweat | swat | sworn | swung | swoop |

sn	snake	sneer	snatch	snitch	snug	snow	snoop
	sneak	snide	snip	snap	snack	snag	snarl
	sniff	snood	snort	snub	snore		

tw	twain	twine	twist	tweet	twig	twin	twill
	twice	twirl	tweed	tweak	twang	twelve	twenty
	twitch						

spl	split	splash	splinter	spleen	splint	splice	splurge

spr	spry	sprout	spring	spruce	sprint	sprang	spray
	sprite	sprig	sprat	sprawl	spree		

str	strip	stripe	string	strung	strand	strike	struck
	strain	street	strong	strait	strange	strap	straw
	stray	streak					

st	fast	most	worst	last	feast	boast	toast
	yeast	first	burst	coast	least	blast	cast
	mast	past					

nk	frank	bank	tank	shrank	drank	Hank	plank
	prank	rank	sank	spank	thank	yank	ink
	think	blink	link	pink	skunk	spunk	junk

ng	bang	sang	sing	wing	swing	bring	spring
	sprang	fling	flung	rung	cling	ding	king
	ping	sling	sting	string	thing	wrung	

nt	want	bent	sent	lent	gent	bunt	brunt
	blunt	plant	plaint	runt	slant	faint	count
	mount	ant	chant	grant	pant	hint	lint

nd	friend	band	bend	wind	wand	sand	send
	lend	spend	blond	stand	strand	brand	grand
	gland	blend	mend	spend	trend	tend	blind

Consonant Combinations (Mixed)

drive	stay	glow	fling	dress	breach	prowl
flight	sleeve	crab	blunt	tray	swim	groan
smite	plait	true	frail	skill	bring	slow
pluck	swing	spool	clash	twig	crop	grip
sneer	skirt	frock	scant	glass	trail	snack
gleam	plate	plank	blond	press	brag	drug
snake	sweep	smell	skate	still	spank	train
graze	bright	gray	free	crib	drip	scab
stand	truck	crush	bless	strike	scrub	strive
crisp	skull	tract	grasp	yelp	held	strip
brisk	cleft	milk	gulf	feast	plant	splash
shelf	dump	sprite	sprout	screech	frisk	boast
film	weld	scrap	bulb	grab	belt	cramp
trust	shrink	stress	plaint	dream	spleen	desk
twin	welt	scalp	tramp	twist	trump	flame
stand	ground	crust	stream	waist	split	blot
state	lump	tweed	blend	scum	flour	wilt
smelt	skip	sport	dream	split	slept	flake
stick	scorn	prow	swept	crime	plump	

More Consonant Combinations

sh

ship	shod	shut	dish	shot
shoe	shin	hash	shop	rash
shelf	show	shed	cash	shell
shift	shave	shore	shun	shake

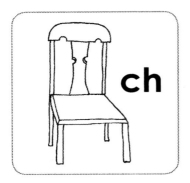

ch

chick	chip	chop	chin
chit	chug	chat	chest
much	rich	catch	hatch
scratch	pitch	hitch	pinch
patch	ranch	latch	chap

th

thimble	thank	thing	thick
thump	both	with	bath

and

than	then	them	this
the	that		

wh

whale	which	whit	whack
whine	while	wheat	wheel
whet	what	white	whim
whiff	whip		

Review of *sh, ch, th* and *wh*

shell	chug	rash	shin	chop	with	both
rich	chin	shelf	chest	fish	thick	chill
shop	chum	hash	this	chin	thin	whim
whip	ship	thing	show	chap	thank	whisk
the	that	them	they	their		

Additional Vowel Sounds

oo	room	soon	roof	cool	drool	broom	food
	pool	boot	spool	loop	toot	moon	tool
	root	shoot	spoon	hoop	boom	loon	school
	droop	coop	pool	fool	noon	troop	roof

oo	stood	foot	took	good	book	cook	look

oi/oy	boil	soil	join	joy	coil	boy	Roy
	toil	point	toy	broil	spoil	coy	

ow/ou	cow	owl	plow	gown	hound	stout	now
	found	down	how	fowl	round	mound	sound
	ground	clown	wow	frown	sour	brow	mouth

Review of additional vowel sounds

boot	choose	show	boon	stoop	cool	thaw
bloom	food	room	book	shoot	noise	broil
smooth	coin	look	spoil	soot	choice	ouch
grouch	cook	house	joint	loud	frown	poise
shout	mooch	jaw	glow	blouse	raw	tow

Vowels Combined with *r*

Rule: Vowels have different sounds when they come before *r*.

ar	bar	part	cart	bark	mark	car	park
	hard	dark	darn	dart	charm	harm	chart
	farm	lark	tar	jar	man	barb	barn
	lard	tart	yarn	start	yard	march	far

or	sort	sport	fork	corn	nor	snort	cork
	cord	north	short	for	or	born	York

ir/er/ur		herd	term	germ	pert	hunter	clerk
		birth	curl	fir	third	fur	stir
		dirt	sir	teacher	flirt	fern	burn
		first	twirl	cur	girl	server	skirt
		shirt	church	spur	firm	turn	summer
		curve	bird	burr			

Teach Anyone To Read: The No-Nonsense Guide

Words That Rhyme

| **all** | wall | ball | all | hall | call | stall |
| | small | tall | gall | mall | pall | fall |

| **ight** | right | fight | light | sight | might | tight | bright |
| | fright | plight | night | blight | flight | slight | bight |

| **ow** | low | flow | bow | row | tow | mow | slow |
| | grow | blow | snow | throw | know | glow | crow |

aw/au	paw	saw	raw	straw	shawl	haul	jaw
	Saul	crawl	claw	yawn	draw	fault	dawn
	lawn	Paul	raw	maul	law	flaw	craw

| **an** | ban | can | fan | man | pan | plan |
| | ran | tan | van | began | Japan | bran |

| **at** | bat | cat | brat | flat | slat | fat | hat |
| | mat | gnat | pat | sat | rat | vat |

| **am** | am | clam | dam | ram | jam |
| | slam | sham | scram | ham | tram |

| **ag** | bag | brag | drag | flag | gag | hag | lag |
| | crag | nag | rag | sag | snag | wag | zigzag |

Teach Anyone To Read: The No-Nonsense Guide

| **ad** | add | bad | cad | dad | fad | gad |
| | glad | had | lad | mad | pad | sad |

ap	cap	chap	zap	clap	gap	lap
	map	nap	rap	sap	slap	snap
	strap	tap	trap			

ot	blot	clot	cot	dot	knot	got
	hot	jot	lot	not	plot	pot
	rot	shot	spot	trot	forgot	slot

| **ob** | Bob | lob | slob | cob | job |
| | mob | rob | snob | sob | blob |

it	bit	fit	hit	kit	knit
	lit	pit	quit	sit	slit
	spit	split	wit	flit	omit

in	bin	din	chin	fin	grin	in
	kin	pin	shin	sin	skin	spin
	thin	tin	twin	win	begin	

| **id** | bid | did | hid | kid | lid |
| | mid | rid | skid | slid | |

ut	mutt	jut	rut	but	cut
	hut	nut	Tut	gut	

un	bun	shun	fun	gun	run
	spun	stun	sun	begun	

up	up	cup	pup	sup	

ud	bud	spud	cud	dud	mud	Jud	thud

eed	heed	deed	seed	need	creed
	bleed	reed	speed	feed	

et	bet	get	jet	let	met
	net	pet	set	wet	vet

en	Ben	den	glen	when	hen
	ken	men	pen	ten	then

ed	bed	bled	fed	fled	led
	red	shed	sled	wed	

old	bold	cold	told	mold	sold
	fold	gold	hold	scold	old

ay	bay	play	clay	ray	day	say	gray
	stray	hay	fray	jay	way	lay	away
	May	delay	pay	display	pray	fray	

eat	beat	peat	cheat	seat	neat	treat
	feat	wheat	heat	defeat	pleat	meat

eam	steam	beam	gleam	cream	scream
	dream	stream	ream	team	seam

eak	weak	streak	beak	squeak	teak	sneak
	leak	bleak	speak	creak	peak	freak

Compound Words

baseball	airport	tonight	moonlight	bookcase
manpower	forecast	highway	shoestring	schoolboy
milkweed	nightgown	downstairs	godfather	eyelash
understand	snowflake	milkman	outcome	sailboat
broadcast	policeman	careless	mailman	anyone
outside	without	uptown	Sunday	inside
someone	cowhand	football	showcase	cottonseed
housefly	downtown	maybe	hallway	fullgrown
lonesome	anyway	cowboy	sunshine	peanut
bowstring	newsboy	password	schooldays	sidewalk
wallpaper	sidestep	anybody	popcorn	birthday
overcook	lighthouse	upstairs	notebook	airplane
bathroom	someday	seaman	tapdance	newspaper
midnight	grapefruit	handbag	snowball	waterfall
tablecloth	schoolroom	grandmother	godmother	within
afternoon				

Practice in Syllabication

Vowel-Consonant-Consonant-Vowel Combinations

abject	aspen	cartoon	altar	expand	fourteen
bedlam	fender	benzene	blanket	expect	chimney
hostage	cancel	ignore	common	insult	butter
sudden	cordial	suffer	embed	lumber	hello
banter	cottage	traffic	correct	pencil	borrow
costume	attend	banner	barrel	hammer	sister
awful	manner	consult	rescue	attic	summer
plastic	walnut	magnet	cellar	postal	napkin
public	beggar	carpet	pumpkin	witness	rabbit
stampede	master	sentence	margin	target	kitten

Vowel-Consonant-Vowel Combinations

never	present	hotel	broken	story	caper
any	icy	ever	avoid	motel	apart
human	over	ideal	lady	direct	amount
July	August	aware	amuse	holy	female
even	lazy	crazy	tulip	before	baby
tiny	solid	committee	cucumber	anticipate	remember
alcohol	abdomen	aggravate	carnival	molasses	amplify
barbecue	important	innocent	entertain	occupy	February
accident	October	November	tomato	December	indirect
September	Halloween	volcano	yesterday	passenger	romantic
domestic	torpedo	carpenter	committee	remainder	surrender
rectify	republic	revolver	establish	advertise	occupant

Prefixes Added to Root Words

Word Wheels are helpful in learning to read these words (see page 165).

en	enter	entire	entrance	enlist	enrage	ensue
	enjoy	enlarge	engulf	engage	enfold	enact
	enable	endear	enforce	enclose	enchant	

ex	examine	external	expert	expense	expel	expect
	exit	exist	exhaust	exhale	exercise	excuse
	except	excite	exact	example	extra	extreme

in	include	insert	income	intact	increase	indeed
	indoor	inhale	insane	inside	insight	inspect
	instep	insult	intend	intuition	inland	

pre	preschool	preview	precede	precinct	prefer
	prefix	prepaid	prepare	present	pretend
	prevail	prevent	prewar	precaution	preside
	predict	preliminary			

con	conform	conceal	convince	concern	contact
	concert	conserve	conclude	contract	concrete
	contain	consume	construct	consist	consent
	connect	confuse			

Teach Anyone To Read: The No-Nonsense Guide

com

compute	compound	compose	complain	compete
complete	compass	compare	commit	commerce
comfort	comment	combine	combat	comic
comma	common			

de

deflate	debate	degrade	decay	deduce	deceive
deliver	decide	declare	decline	decrease	deduct
defeat	defend	deform	delay	demand	delight

dis

disown	disable	distress	disagree	dispute
disarm	disrupt	disband	discard	discharge
disclose	discount	discuss	disease	disgust
dislike	dismiss	distrust		

pro

protest	provoke	protect	propose	pronoun
promote	program	profile	produce	procure
proceed	proclaim	proportion		

re

redo	recall	relearn	receive	remain	record
reduce	remove	report	respect	reform	replace
retire	reward	regain	refresh	resort	reproduce

un

unsure	unprepared	unwashed	undone	unclear
unusual	unhappy	unfold	unfit	unfair
uneasy	undress	uncut	uncover	uncommon
unclean	unborn	unarmed		

Suffixes Added To Roots

s	milks	pants	stains	rests	rolls	fails	seems
ing	milking	panting	staining	resting	rolling	failing	seeming
ed	milked	panted	stained	rested	rolled	failed	seemed

er	poorer	nearer	weaker	deeper	darker	dearer	softer
est	poorest	nearest	weakest	deepest	darkest	dearest	softest

ance	distance	clearance	performance	instance	ignorance
	finance	entrance	assistance	appearance	allowance
	annoyance	abundance	reliance		

ous	gracious	infamous	glorious	poisonous	nervous
	previous	murderous	mountainous	marvelous	joyous
	famous	enormous	dangerous		

able	probable	likable	remarkable	available
	fashionable	enjoyable	suitable	desirable
	dependable	comfortable	considerable	capable
	agreeable			

ent	complement	supplement	dependent	present
	permanent	intelligent	innocent	incident
	resident	excellent	different	content
	comment	dissident		

ly

suddenly	friendly	sadly	quietly	gently
justly	yearly	highly	weekly	hardly
warmly	gladly	sweetly	freshly	softly
freely	richly	poorly	fairly	deeply
plainly	closely	nearly	openly	lovely

ness

business	easiness	lowness	tallness	whiteness
softness	highness	greatness	darkness	dampness
plainness	sweetness	madness	illness	likeness
sadness	weakness	goodness	sickness	wellness

ment

achievement	pavement	movement	investment
shipment	treatment	excitement	enlargement
engagement	deportment	contentment	betterment
assignment	appointment	amusement	amazement
agreement	entertainment	instrument	

tion

vacation	objection	solution	donation
exception	correction	construction	connection
collection	carnation	attraction	adoption
ration	motion	action	

ful

lawful	skillful	restful	powerful
peaceful	painful	joyful	harmful
handful	grateful	frightful	faithful
cupful	cheerful	bashful	awful

Common Antonyms (Opposites)

sick	well	up	down
yes	no	boy	girl
walk	run	thin	fat
sit	stand	open	shut
love	hate	cat	dog
big	little	give	take
he	she	near	far
hot	cold	weak	strong
lost	found	wild	tame
light	dark	remember	forget
awake	asleep	happy	sad
before	after	mother	father
come	go	narrow	wide
black	white	day	night
noisy	quiet	sour	sweet
dead	alive	wet	dry
front	back	brother	sister
dirty	clean	early	late
empty	full	light	dark
north	south	off	on
laugh	cry	true	false
man	woman	strong	weak
top	bottom	in	out
sharp	dull	friend	enemy
young	old	pretty	ugly

Common Homonyms

(Words that sound the same but have different meanings)

be	bee	knows	nose	
reed	read	sea	see	
threw	through	mail	male	
new	knew	right	write	
hair	hare	pane	pain	
dear	deer	I	eye	
beet	beat	meat	meet	
add	ad	berry	bury	
ale	ail	know	no	
or	ore	cheep	cheap	
flair	flare	tail	tale	
gate	gait	night	knight	
feet	feat	sail	sale	
bow	bough	brake	break	
bear	bare	rode	road	
pail	pale	there	their	
week	weak	piece	peace	
ant	aunt	pair	pair	pare
blew	blue	for	four	fore
ate	eight	merry	marry	Mary
red	read	to	too	two
throne	thrown	so	sew	sow
hear	here	sent	scent	cent
peek	peak	do	dew	due

Common Heteronyms

(Words that are spelled the same, but pronounced differently)

absent	perfect	appropriate	reject
congress	transplant	estimate	wound
minute	affiliate	rebel	buffet
subordinate	deliberate	upset	insert
abuse	present	approximate	resume
contact	transport	excuse	close
moped	alternate	record	intimate
suspect	discount	use	sewer
accent	primer	articulate	compact
convict	triplicate	graduate	invalid
object	annex	refuse	subject
tear	duplicate	wind	compound
address	read	bow	lead
coordinate	underestimate	increase	

Selected Words with Several Meanings

drop	fall, stop, small amount
electrify	shock, thrill
entertain	delight, consider
examine	study, test
faculty	talent, teachers
fence	railing, partition, bootleg, swordfight
firm	solid, company
follow	trail, pursue, obey
forge	build, counterfeit, smelter, progress
freeze	chill, stiffen
grasp	hold, control, understand
grub	dig, toil, larva, food

harvest	gather, crop
just	precisely, only, fair
list	record, slant
manual	handbook, by hand
origin	beginning, root
peer	equal, look
pool	small body of water, combine
race	hurry, group of people
responsible	accountable, trustworthy
rock	swing, stone

scrap	fight, particle, waste
spot	stain, recognize
stage	perform, level, platform
straight	direct, honest, conventional
switch	a strap, beat, to change
tape	record, sealing material for papers and equipment
worn	used, tired
vault	safe, tomb, jump
volume	quantity, a book
watch	view, guard, instrument for telling time

Selected Idioms

For additional idioms, see page 83 and *Word Play, A Dictionary of Idioms,* by Lillie Pope

Beard the lion	Burn the candle at both ends	Cock and bull story
Beat about the bush	Bury the hatchet	Come in handy
Behind his/her back	Butt in	Cook his goose
Below the belt	By and large	Cool as a cucumber
Beside myself	By the skin of my teeth	Count your chickens before they are hatched
Beside the point	By the way	Crack a joke
Better half	Call up	Cream of the crop
Between the devil and the deep sea	Carry on	Cry wolf
Big hand	Carry the ball	Dark horse
Big shot	Catch fire	Dead as a doornail
Birds of a feather	Catch his eye	Dirty look
Bite your head off	Catch red-handed	Do away with
Blind date	Chain smoker	Dog-tired
Blow off steam	Chalk up	Doll up
Bone to pick	Change hands	Double-cross
Bosom friends	Change your mind	Down to earth
Break away	Check in	Draw the line
Break the ice	Check out	Drop by (drop in)
Bring home the bacon	Chew the fat	Drop in the bucket
Bring to mind	Chin up	Drop off
Brush-off	Chips are down	Dutch treat
	Close call	Eat your heart out

Eat her words

Eat your cake and have it too

Elbow grease

Face the music

Fair and square

Fall apart

Far cry

Farfetched

Feather in her cap

Feather my nest

Feel blue

Feel it in my bones

Fence sitter

Fifty-fifty

Finger in every pot (pie)

Fit as a fiddle

Flash in the pan

Fly in the ointment

Fool around

Foot the bill

For a song

Forty winks

From A to Z

Get even with

Get in touch with

Get it off your chest

Get on my nerves

Get the upper hand

Get under my skin

Get wind of

Ghost of a chance

Give in

Give the cold shoulder

Give you a piece of my mind

Go-getter

Go out of his way

Go straight

Go to bat for

Go to pot

Half-baked

Halfhearted

Handle with kid gloves

Hand-to-mouth

Have a bone to pick

Have a lot on the ball

Have a screw loose

Have cold feet

Have irons in the fire

Have my hands full

Head over heels

Hold back

Holding the bag

Hold your horses

Hold your tongue

Hot air

In a nutshell

In clover

In dutch

In her right mind

In the doghouse

In the nick of time

Jot down

Jump at

Keep house

Keep in touch with

Keep your head

Keep the wolf from the door

Kill two birds with one stone

Know the ropes

Ladies' man

Lay off

Leave no stone unturned

Left-handed compliment

Leg to stand on

Lend an ear

Like a fish out
of water

Look down on

Lose his shirt

Make a clean breast

Make a mountain
out of a molehill

Make believe

Make ends meet

Make eyes at

Make no bones about

Makes my blood boil

Meet halfway

Monkey around with

Nip in the bud

Nose to the
grindstone

Old hand

On its last legs

On the dot

On the whole

Out of the question

Pay through the nose

Play the market

Play with fire

Pulling my leg

Put her foot in
her mouth

Put two and
two together

Put your foot down

Raw deal

Right-hand man

Rub someone the
wrong way

Run across

Save face

Say a mouthful

Scare the daylights
out of

See eye to eye

Skate on thin ice

Slip through
my fingers

Smell a rat

Sneeze at

Split hairs

Step on the gas

Stick your neck out

Stiff upper lip

Straight from the
horse's mouth

Straight from the shoulder

Stretch a point

Strike while the iron is hot

Stuffed shirt

Take the bull by the horns

Talk shop

Talk through his hat

Talk turkey

Through thick and thin

Throw in the sponge

Thumbs up

To be of age

Tom, Dick and Harry

Tongue lashing

Turn over a new leaf

Under his thumb

Upset the applecart

Under the weather

White elephant

Win hands down

Sample Comprehension Skills Exercises

Some of the following sentences are true, some are false and some are statements of opinion. Can you tell which are which?

1. Cats chase mice.

2. Most people are right handed.

3. The sun sets in the west.

4. The sky is pink.

5. All dogs have shaggy black hair.

6. A window always has two panes of glass.

7. President Bush was the wisest president we ever had.

8. A morning cup of coffee is an excellent stimulant.

9. A cigarette a day is not harmful to health.

10. Mark Twain was a funny man.

11. Vitamin C helps avoid many illnesses.

12. This book will undoubtedly become a best-seller.

13. The giraffe has a very long neck.

14. Dogs meow.

15. The sea is salty.

16. A school contains classrooms.

17. Australia is in the southern hemisphere.

18. A magic marker is a ballpoint pen.

19. The sky is cloudy all the time.

20. The weather in Washington, D.C., is quite comfortable in the summer.

21. My mother is the most beautiful woman in the world.

22. Vanilla ice cream is more delicious than chocolate.

23. Down pillows are more comfortable than polyurethane.

24. Dr. Smith is a fine dentist.

25. The sun rises in the west.

26. The moon is blue.

27. A ping-pong ball can be used in playing golf.

28. Canoes have sails.

29. Purple is a color.

30. Kansas City is in the United States.

Who? What? When? Where? Why? How?

Find the answers to these questions in the following sentences:

1. Frieda Geller sometimes worked during the morning at the clinic to help the staff by keeping attendance records of the children who came.

2. Driving down Neptune Avenue at 8:00 A.M., the policeman carefully watched for cars that might be speeding.

3. The Atlantic Ocean last year flooded the beach at Sea Gate with loud crashing waves due to a major hurricane.

4. Early in the morning Grandfather always prepared hot oatmeal in the kitchen for breakfast for his grandchildren.

5. The children clapped loudly because they enjoyed today's concert and dance recital at the Academy of Music.

6. Early in the morning, the firemen drove out of the fire station quickly to put out the big fire.

7. To build a house, the builder uses plans drawn up by the architect in advance.

8. With email, people can now send messages to friends and business associates all over the world instantly.

9. John watched the local news on his TV set on Monday evening to learn about the weekend's weather.

10. To help make the health fair a success in May, the children painted squares for the patchwork quilt to be displayed at the table.

NOPQRSTUV
WXYZABCDE
FGHIJKLMN
OPQRSTUVW
XYZABCDEF
GHIJKLMNO
PQRSTUVWX
YZABCDEFG
HIJKLMNOPQ
RSTUVWXYZ

Appendix

Appendix

What to Do About Common Reading Errors and Difficulties

Frequently Asked Questions

Helpful Resources

Glossary

Common Reading Errors and Difficulties

- **If your student is confused about where to start reading** on the page, he needs practice to build the habit of reading from left to right. Can the student consistently distinguish between left and right? If he is hesitant or unsure about the difference, he must first be taught. Putting a watch, a loose rubber band or a bracelet around his right wrist will help. Play Simon Says, making the instructions very simple: Touch your right eye, your left ear, etc. If the student has difficulty, demonstrate the correct response as you give the instructions, standing or sitting beside the student so that your left and right match his. If you face him, he may become more confused.

After the student has learned left from right, he must be given a great deal of practice in moving his eyes from left to right across the printed page. Drawing a line down the left side of the page, an arrow across the page or a line under the first letter will help remind the student where to start reading. Printing the first letter of each word in colored crayon will remind the student to sound out from left to right. You will find additional exercises in early grade workbooks.

- **If your student has difficulty in learning the letter shapes,** remember to use all of his senses in teaching him. This is a common problem for someone who has never advanced beyond the primer or pre-primer level, no matter what grade he is now in. Use cut-out letters in different materials, such as felt, sandpaper and velvet. Have the student touch them and trace them with his fingers, as well as shape the letters in clay and out of pipe cleaners. Have the student combine the letters into words, and say the words. (See pages 23 and 130–131 for additional suggestions.)

Tracing the solid letters and then the outline letters will help the student learn the letter shape:

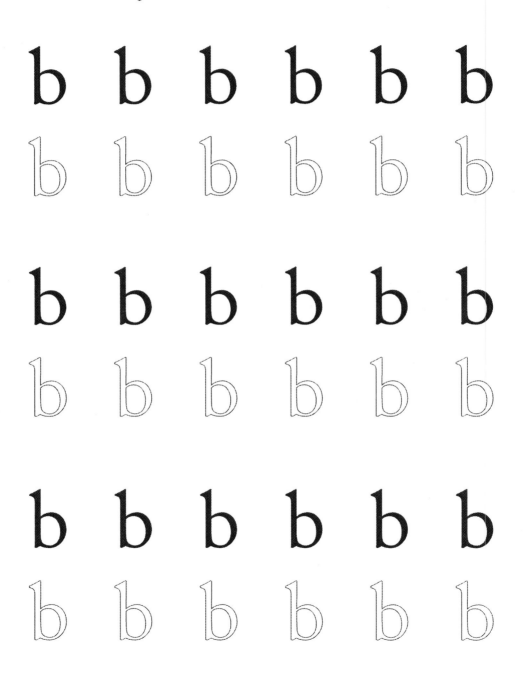

- **If your student reverses words or letters,** or reads them backwards, he is actually failing to read from left to right. This is a common problem, and requires special attention. Patient practice in sounding out letters in sequence from left to right will usually solve this difficulty. The most frequently reversed words are: *saw, was, on, no, not, ton, pot, top, now, won.*

- **If your student guesses and substitutes words,** the reading material is too difficult. Give the student easier material to read, and be patient. When he guesses or substitutes, urge him to sound out the words; however, try not to stop the student too frequently. On occasion, when the substitution does not substantially alter the meaning of the material, it may be overlooked in order to add fluency to the reading.

- **If your student omits words and letters,** he is not yet reading smoothly. His eye may skip a word, or letters within a word, now and then, and he does not read phrases well enough to absorb the meaning of all the words. Such errors should be called to the student's attention as they occur; as skill and fluency increase, this problem should disappear. Practice in reading phrases, so that the eye takes in several words at each stop, will help in overcoming this difficulty. (See pages 166–167 for suggestions on reading phrases.)

- **If your student reads word by word,** as though the words are in a list, he still finds each new word difficult and is unable to read phrases or comprehend easily what he is reading. The mechanics of reading are still a problem to this student. He needs practice in reading phrases and in reading with expression. Expose the reading material one phrase at a time, so that the student is encouraged to read the whole phrase, and then move on to the next. This gives the student confidence in his ability and practice in oral reading, and helps the student relax. With increased skill and relaxation, oral reading will become expressive and less mechanical. It is also helpful to have this student read interesting books and stories at a lower reading level. Reading that material fluently and enjoyably will give him confidence to progress to more challenging material after a while.

- **If your student forms words with his lips** during silent reading, he will have difficulty learning to read quickly. Explain that it is not helpful to say the words when reading them. Let the student hold a pencil in his mouth while reading silently, to prevent the lip motion. If, however, the student resists giving up the lip reading, do not make an issue of it. Eventually he will stop moving his lips, when he no longer needs to do so.

• **If your student repeatedly loses his place** while reading, let him hold a ruler or a piece of paper under the line being read. After a while, try removing it. If he still loses his place, let him continue to use the guide. Remove it when it is no longer needed.

• **If your student confuses letters** such as b/d, p/q, t/f, m/w and u/n, she is confusing letters that have the same shape but face in different directions, or in the case of h/n and t/l, that have slight differences.

In the case of letters that have the same shapes, print each letter large and have the student trace it. Emphasize the different directions in which they point. Associate the letter shapes with concrete images: for example, b and d have flagpoles, p and q have long tails; b has a big belly; m has two mountains. Associate key words with each letter. Make use, too, of the sensory aids suggested in the section on learning letters.

Have the student circle every b in the following list:

d	d	b	b	d	b	d	d	b
b	b	d	d	d	b	b	d	d
b	b	d	b	d	d	b	b	b
d	d	d	b	b	d	b	d	d
b	b	b	d	d	d	b	b	d
d	b	b	d	b	d	d	b	b
b	d	d	b	d	d	b	b	d

If, after you have pointed out the differences, the student continues to confuse a particular pair of letters, teach one of the letters and temporarily ignore the other. Concentrate on the first letter until the student knows it automatically. Then set it aside and teach the second letter until the student knows it very well. Now bring back the first, and let the student work on both letters together. For a short time he may still confuse them slightly: he will soon learn to discriminate between the two.

Appendix

What to Do About
Common Reading
Errors and Difficulties

Frequently Asked Questions

Helpful Resources

Glossary

Frequently Asked Questions

1. "I teach a third-grade class of twenty-five children. Three of these children need special help in order to learn to read. How can I help them without neglecting the rest of the class?"

Many teachers have this problem. It can be solved in several ways. If possible, refer them to the resource room, where the resource room teacher can attend to their needs in small group instruction. If this is not possible, arrange to have a trained volunteer tutor to work with each child twice a week, under your supervision. This is no great burden to you: you describe the specific needs of each child to the tutor and provide materials that will be helpful for instruction. If possible, plan to spend a few minutes each day with every student in the class. The minutes spent with the most needy students will be very productive.

2. "One of my students seems to have trouble understanding some of the simplest words when I speak to him—words like *up, down, in front of, behind, over* and *under.* Is this possible? Does it matter? What can be done?"

Some students who have difficulty in learning to read have not yet learned the words that describe relationships. If she does not know *up* and *down* or *over* and *under*, she will have difficulty distinguishing between the letters *b* and *p*. She may have acquired a simple vocabulary to talk about things and actions, but she cannot describe relationships that involve such concepts as *next to, underneath, because* and *if*, and as a result, learning is difficult.

Play games in which the student places an object *over, under* and *next to* a table. Draw pictures of a hat *on, between, through, over* and *under* a chair. Have the student draw pictures illustrating the use of the terms you want to teach.

3. "My student seems to hear perfectly well, but she confuses some of the sounds. For example, she can't seem to hear the difference between *room* and *loom*. How do you explain this?"

Even when some people listen, they do not discriminate between certain sounds. An individual may speak a dialect of English in which letters are given different sounds (for example, saying *pin* for *pen*). If the student's first language is foreign, she may retain some accents and pronunciations of that language (a Spanish speaker may say *sheep* for *ship*). Sometimes an individual may hear the differences between the sounds, but has not yet learned to say them differently and clearly (saying *free* for *three*).

If the problem is simply one of dialect or foreign accent, it is best to spend your time on other problems.

Students who have difficulty in differentiating sounds need much exercise in listening for particular sounds, in recognizing differences between different sounds (a doorbell and a cat's meow), and then between similar sounds (a doorbell and a telephone ring). They should listen for rhyming words, and have fun with rhymes. And finally, they should be given exercises to practice distinguishing between words that sound very different (*mark* and *cow*, for example), and between words that sound more similar (*mark* and *bark*).

4. "I teach my students to say the names of the letters when they try to sound out a new word. My colleague says that that is the wrong thing to do. What do you say?"

Your friend is correct. If the student says the name of each letter, she will find it very dfficult to sound out a new word. For example, suppose that she tries to read the word *dog*. Using your method, she will say *dee, oh, gee*. She will then try to put them together (or blend them) into a word, and say *deeohgee*, which doesn't sound at all like *dog*. It is much easier for the student to concentrate on the sound of the letter, rather than its name. She should then say *d o g*, blending the sounds together to say *dog*, without having to drop any extra sounds.

5. "I have a student who skips words, puts in words that are not there, has trouble finding the next line, and in general, has difficulty in working in an orderly manner. What should I do?"

This is a common problem. This student needs help in working her way across the page in a systematic way. Encourage her to point to words with her finger, or point to words yourself with a pencil. Place a sheet of paper or a ruler under the line that is being read to block out the remainder of the page. She needs such structure to assist her until she becomes skillful enough to work without aids.

6. "One of my students is a boy of 16 who cannot read the simplest first-grade reader. How can he be helped?"

If he is to be helped now, the instruction must begin at a basic level. He must learn to sound out letters, read sight words and follow the sequence of skills as every other beginning reader does. He needs more reassurance than a younger learner, because his years of failure have convinced him that he cannot learn. Sometimes older boys will insist that they do not want to work with "baby books" or "baby stuff." They must be reminded that no one can climb to the top of a staircase without starting at the bottom step—and that eventually, if they persist, they will get to the top.

7. "One student in my class always finds excuses for avoiding work. What can I do to get him to settle down with his reading?"

If you plan your sessions with the student well, the reading will be focused on subjects that interest him, and the activities will include games that are enjoyable, even for practice that is usually dry and repetitive.

The best thing to do in this case is to tell the student simply that if he does not settle down to work on the planned activities, you are sorry that you will have to replace him with another student. Offer him a choice of two activities, or the privilege of selecting which of the planned activities he wishes to do first, or the privilege of playing games during the last five minutes of the session—but he must work according to your plan until then.

8. "Some of the instructors in my school give the students stars, prizes or cookies when they do good work. I think it is dreadful to bribe children in this way. What do you think?"

Bribes are dreadful; rewards and incentives are great. Praise, a smile, a pat on the back, a star, a cookie or a prize is a reward for a job well done, and encourages the student to work for more success and more rewards. They should be viewed as rewards, not as bribes.

9. "Many of my students love comic books, though they cannot read. Is it wrong for me use comic books as reading matter?"

Use comic books by all means. Use any reading matter that interests your students. Preview the comic books to be sure that the words are printed legibly, and that they are not too difficult for the students.

Some instructors cover up the printed words in the "balloons" that accompany the pictures and substitute words provided by their students who have made up their own stories based on the pictures. The instructor prints the dictated dialogue in the balloons, and presto…the student has dictated a comic book!

10. "Kevin comes from South Carolina and is always making mistakes in his speech. He omits sounds and pronounces words incorrectly, and I know that he will have trouble getting a good job if he continues to talk that way. Although he is only 8 years old, I feel that I should teach him to speak correctly. Don't you agree?"

No. Kevin has a long way to go before he need worry about getting a good job. The errors that you describe are not "errors" but are part of the dialect that is correct and appropriate in the community that he comes from. Although standard English may eventually be helpful to him in getting a good job, right now it is not necessary to teach him your way of speaking. Your goal is to help him learn to read. Do not correct his speech now, or you will be spending too much time on that and not on reading. Since he hears standard English spoken by his teachers at school and on television all the time, you may be confident that he understands "proper" English. Eventually he will modify his own speech, if he finds it necessary and helpful.

Speaking of dialects, have you thought that perhaps your own speech is a dialect, and that it differs from the English spoken in Boston, Philadelphia, Brooklyn or Chicago? All of us speak some dialect of English that will seem a bit strange to others.

11. "Maria had difficulty learning the short a sound. That is all we worked on every time we met, for two months. I had her read lists of words, such as act, all period, every period. Now she seems reluctant to come to our tutoring sessions. And to tell you the truth, I am very bored, too. If repetition is so important in teaching a reluctant learner, why did it have this effect on Maria—and on me?"

Repetition is important, but monotony will ruin the student's desire to learn. Practice must be presented in a variety of ways, with never a possibility of boredom. Plan for the same skill to be practiced with different materials, games and activities, and using all the senses.

12. "Martin is doing very nicely, but I worry about him. His shoes have holes in them, he never has a tissue when his nose is running and I am certain he does not have a good breakfast before coming to school. What can I do?"

If his nose is running, hand him a tissue. Otherwise, report all of these problems to your supervisor, who will try to do something about them. Thank goodness he is doing nicely in his learning.

13. "I am reluctant to play games with the child I teach because they take so much time. Don't you think I can accomplish more without games?"

No. Games add pleasure and variety to the lesson. Prior to receiving instruction from you, your student was uncomfortable with reading. Be patient. Progress will seem slow, but games will eventually help the child learn more quickly.

14. "I play games all the time, and I try to make sure that I lose all the time, so that my student will feel good about winning. Isn't that a good idea?"

No. Never try to fool your student by "losing on purpose." He will see through you, and feel that you lack confidence in his ability to win or to lose gracefully. In addition, he will lose confidence in your ability to deal with him honestly. Play it straight.

On occasion, you will find a student who is fiercely competitive and is not a graceful loser. With this student, it is desirable to play games in which he competes with himself, each time trying to match or exceed his own previous score. This practice encourages his progress and rewards his success, while it discourages the student from using his thirst for competition as a weapon against the loser (who may very well be himself.)

15. "Jamal points to each word with his finger. I remember that when I was in school, the teacher used to slap my wrist for doing that. Yet when I stop him from pointing, Jamal loses his place."

Many teachers still object to pointing, just as your teacher did when you were a child. Nevertheless, Jamal has a special problem. His eye darts around the page and he loses his place unless he can use his finger or some other pointer. He should be permitted to do this until he reads fluently enough not to need this assistance. When he no longer needs to point with his finger, he will stop doing it.

16. "Emily's handwriting is awful. The letters are uneven and hard to read, and the lines wave all over the place. How can I help her?"

Some students have difficulty in coordinating their hand movements, and their penmanship is correspondingly poor. There are several ways in which you can help.

Since you understand that Emily's handwriting is poor because of a problem of coordination (rather than because she is careless or intentionally sloppy), then you will understand that you cannot expect perfect writing from her—and you will be able to tolerate her unevenness more easily. She needs structure and assistance to form letters properly and to write evenly. Give her as many guides and aids as you can. Use lined paper, with wide spaces between the lines. She may have to trace the letters, and she may need boxes in which to shape letters. Let her have whatever she needs.

Letting her type her assignments on a computer on occasion will give her the satisfaction of turning out good-looking material while she struggles to improve her handwriting!

17. "My friend tells me that volunteerism is a means of exploitation—that it demeans the volunteers and places them in an inferior position, implying that their work is worth nothing in the job market. What do you think?"

To volunteer in a helping field is an act that should be respected and encouraged. People volunteer for many different reasons. Some volunteers are women who, for various reasons, have not pursued careers or have been out of the job market. Individuals who do not have recent job experience often have feelings similar to those of students who have failed in reading: they lack self-confidence.

Successful volunteers bolster their sense of self-worth by learning that they are able to help others. They can explore working in different fields that had seemed impenetrable without prior experience, and many have used their volunteer experience to further their professional training and obtain paying jobs. Individuals who are not interested in paid employment—and these people do exist—may remain in the volunteer program, enriching it with their experience and helping train a new corps of volunteers.

For retired persons, working part-time as a volunteer is a way to make a contribution to society, to feel needed and to continue to be productive.

Volunteers cannot replace the paid professional, but they are invaluable in making the professional's work more effective.

Appendix

What to Do About
Common Reading
Errors and Difficulties

Frequently Asked Questions

Helpful Resources

Glossary

Helpful Resources

Following are lists of publishers and reference materials that you will find helpful. It is important to remember that the publishing world is at this time in a state of constant flux; publishing houses are consolidated, programs are dropped, and new programs are developed. For the most current information, I suggest that you call the "800" number of publishers for their current catalogs, and also check out their listings on the Internet. If you are searching for a book that is out of print, several booksellers, including Amazon.com, Abebooks.com, Barnesandnoble.com, and Deepdiscount.com may have the used book you are looking for, often at a discounted price.

Annotated List of Publishers of Materials That Emphasize Reading Skills and Vocabulary Development

Students in reading programs need assistance in developing specific reading skills, as outlined in the text. The publishers listed here produce many materials that are helpful in reading skills development, and many also list literature to read for pleasure:

For All Age Levels

Those marked * are particularly helpful with adults and young adults.

* Contemporary Books, Inc. (McGraw-Hill Professional),
  2 Penn Plaza, New York, NY 10121; 212/904-2000;
  http://www.mhprofessional.com/

  Number Power

Educators Publishing Service, PO Box 9031,
Cambridge, MA, 02139-9031; 800/435-7728;
http://www.epsbooks.com/

Excellent materials; a <u>must</u> in a remedial program. Particularly noteworthy are:

Primary Phonics
Recipe For Reading, by Nina Traub
The Gillingham Manual & Materials

* Fearon Books, available through Pearson/AGS Globe Books Pearson Education, PO Box 2500, Lebanon, IN, 46052; 800/328-2560; http://www.agsglobe.com/

Books about geography, culture, nature, science and the arts.

Work Tales:
Ten titles dealing with problems in the workplace, with discussion questions after each chapter. Reading level 0–4, adult, new reader materials.

Heinemann (division of Greenwood Publishing Group, Inc.)
Heinemann, P. O. Box 6926, Portsmouth, NH 03802-6926; 800/225-5800; http://www.heinemann.com/

International Reading Association, http://www.reading.org/; 800/336-7323; 302/731-1600   Catalog of Professional Resources

* Jamestown Education (McGraw-Hill, Glencoe Online); 800/872-7323; http://www.glencoe.com/gln/jamestown/index.php4

These books are recommended for pre-reading, during-reading and after-reading activities, and to develop interpretive reading skills:

Skimming And Scanning

* New Readers Press (division of ProLiteracy Worldwide); 1320 Jamesville Ave., Syracuse, NY 13210; 800/448-8878; http://www.newreaderspress.com/

Collections of stories at first and second grade reading, in addition to material on skills instruction. Particularly helpful with adults and young adults.

Timeless Tales (reading levels 2-3)

* Phoenix Learning Resources, 800/228-9345; http://www.phoenixlearningresources.com/

Good source of remedial materials.

Programmed Reading, by Sullivan and Buchanan
(reading level K-6; interest level K-6/ESL)

Reading Readiness, by Sullivan and Buchanan
(reading level preschool-1; interest level preschool-1,ESL)

Programmed Reading For Adults, by Sullivan and Buchanan
(reading level 1-6; interest level 7-adult)

SRA/McGraw-Hill, 220 East Danieldale Road, Desoto, TX 75115-2490; 888/772-4543;
https://www.sraonline.com/

The Merrill Linguistic Reading Program and *The Merrill Phonics Skilltext Series*
are basic to a program for disabled readers.
Reading Level: Beginning to 6; Interest Level: All.

The Open Court Reading Program is a well-established developmental reading
program, based on a phonics approach, and has been successfully used in many
school systems.

* Steck-Vaughn, A Harcourt Achieve Imprint, Harcourt Achieve, Attn: Cust Serv.

6277 Sea Harbor Dr., Orlando, FL 32887; 800-531-5015;
http://steckvaughn.harcourtachieve.com/en-US/steckvaughn.htm

Skills instruction, teaching critical thinking

Wonders Of Science Series (Level 7–12)
History Of Our World
Writing Excellence (Level K–Adult)

These books contain maps, photographs and graphs, and integrate reading
and writing activities with vocabulary development and critical thinking.

* Wilson Language Training, 47 Old Webster Road, Oxford, MA 01540; 508/368-2399;
http://www.wilsonlanguage.com/

Wilson Reading System: a helpful program based on skills development for
disabled readers; interest level 5–adult.

Publishers of Literature to Inspire, Encourage and Open the World of Reading for Beginning and Disabled Readers of All Ages

The number of books available for the beginning reader has skyrocketed in recent years, particularly in the field of children's books. It is impossible to enumerate here the many excellent books that can be helpful and pleasurable for your students. Have confidence in your own judgment of books that you find to be interesting and attractive. Your local librarian can be helpful, as can catalogues from the following publishers. Ask for catalogues of literature-based reading materials.

Those marked with * in this section are particularly helpful with adults and young adults.

* Avon Books, Harper Collins Children's Books,
  1350 Ave. of the Americas, New York, NY 10019; 212/261-6500;
  http://www.harpercollinschildrens.com/HarperChildrens/Kids/

  Award-winning books by notable authors for children and young adults, including a sizable list of multicultural books.

Children's Book Press, 2211 Mission Street, San Francisco, CA 94110; 415/821-3080;
http://www.childrensbookpress.org/

Award-winning children's picture books helping to create a literature of inclusion.

Children's Press (Franklin Watt), Scholastic,
557 Broadway, New York, New York 10012, 212-343-6100
http://librarypublishing.scholastic.com/

Early childhood non-fiction, Spanish-language titles.

Bantam Dell, Random House Inc.,
1745 Broadway, New York, NY 10019; 212/782-9000;
http://www.randomhouse.com/kids/index.pperl

Inexpensive paperback adaptations of children's classics, including biographies of Abraham Lincoln, Frederick Douglass and John F. Kennedy;
reading level 2-8; interest level: children, early teens.

Greenwillow Books, Harper Collins Publishers,
1350 Avenue of the Americas, New York, NY 10019; 212/261-6500;
http://www.harpercollins.com/imprints/index.aspx?imprintid=517996

Harper-Collins Publishers,
1350 Avenue of the Americas, New York, NY 10019; 212/261-6500;
http://www.harpercollins.com/

Houghton Mifflin Publishing Co., 222 Berkeley Street, Boston, MA 02116;
617/351-5000; http://www.hmco.com/

Lee and Low Books, 95 Madison Ave., Suite 1205, New York, NY 10016;
212/779-4400; http://www.leeandlow.com/

Award-winning publisher specializing in multicultural themes.

Literacy Partners, Inc.,. 30 East 33rd St., New York, NY 10016, 212/725-9200;
http://www.literacypartners.org/

A not-for-profit organization, provides free community-based adult and family
literacy programs.

Macmillan/McGraw-Hill Publishing Co.,
1221 Ave. of the Americas, New York, NY 10020; 212/512-2000;
http://www.macmillanmh.com/ (contact list: http://www.mhschool.com/contactus/
    region.php3?id=1025)

Macmillan/McGraw-Hill's free online resources are for teachers, students and
parents, plus product information for grades K through 8.

William Morrow, an imprint of Harper-Collins Publishers,
10 East 53rd St., New York, NY 10022; 212/261-6500;
http://www.harpercollins.com/imprints/index.aspx?imprintid=518003

Orchard Books, The Watts Publishing Group
(a division of Hachette Children's Books), 338 Euston Road, LONDON, NW1 3BH;
020 7873 6000; http://www.wattspub.co.uk/

Pearson Learning Group (K-12),
135 South Mount Zion Road, P.O. Box 2500, Lebanon, IN 46052; 800/526-9907;
http://www.pearsonlearning.com/

This group encompasses many education companies, with material for all ages.

* Readers Digest, Reader's Digest Road, Pleasantville, NY 10570-7000; 800/304-2807;
http://www.rd.com/

Success in reading one of the Readers Digest simple books is a source of enormous
pleasure for a beginning reader, particularly an adult or a young adult.

Scholastic, Inc., 557 Broadway, New York, NY 10012-3999; 800/724-6527;
http://www.scholastic.com/

Inexpensive paperbacks, K–8.

Scott, Foresman and Co., Pearson Education,
One Lake Street, Upper Saddle River, NJ 07458; 201/236-7000;
http://scottforesman.com/

Silver Moon Press, 381 Park Avenue South, New York, NY 10016; 800/874-3320;
http://www.silvermoonpress.com/

Silver Moon Press is a young, growing children's book publisher. In just a few
years they have created nearly 50 titles in such areas as test preparation, science,
multiculture, and biographies. Their biggest and most exciting area of study,
however, is historical fiction.

Simon and Schuster
1230 Avenue of the Americas,New York, NY 10020, 212/698-7000;
http://www.simonsays.com/

Biography series, with vocabulary and interpretive reading activities:
American Biographies
World Biographies

Viking-Penguin USA, 375 Hudson St., New York, NY 10014; 212/366-2000;
http://us.penguingroup.com/
For customer service: 800/331-4624, orders: 800/526-0275

Publishers of Books of Special Interest for ESL Students and Adults with Significant Reading Delays

Addison-Wesley/Longman Publishing Group,
75 Arlington St.,Suite 300, Boston, MA, 02116; 617/848-6000
http://www.awprofessional.com/index.asp?rl=1

Cambridge University Press Distribution Center,
100 Brook Hill Drive, Nyack, NY 10994; 845/353-7500;
http://www.cambridge.org/us/

Task Reading by Evelyn Davies, Norman Whitney, Meredith Pike-Baky, Laurie Blass;
Paperback (ISBN-13:9780521358101 I ISBN-10:0521358108)

Longman Publishing Group, (Addison, Wesley Longman), Pearson Education,
One Lake Street, Upper Saddle River, NJ 07458, 201/236-7000;
http://www.longman.com/

Problem Solving: Critical Thinking And Communication Skills,
by Linda W. Little and Ingrid Greenberg

New Readers Press (Pro-Literacy Worldwide),
1320 Jamesville Avenue, Syracuse, NY 13210; 800- 448-8878;
http://www.newreaderspress.com/

Living In America Series, by Rosanne Keller

Newbury House Publishers,div. of Heinle, a div. of Thompson Higher Education,
10 Davis Drive, Belmont, CA 94002; 800-354-9706; http://www.thomsonedu.com/

Prentice Hall Regents, 113 Sylvan Ave., Englewood Cliffs, NJ 07632;
800/562-0245; http://www.prenticehall.com/

Scott, Foresman and Co., Pearson Education,
One Lake Street, Upper Saddle River, NJ 07458, 201/236-7000; 800/552-2259;
http://scottforesman.com/

Steck-Vaughn, Harcourt Achieve,
Attn: Customer Service, 5th Floor, 6277 Sea Harbor Drive, Orlando, FL 32887,
800/531-5015; http://steckvaughn.harcourtachieve.com/

Wonders of Science Series—Reading level 7-12

Bibliographies of Books
Useful in Reading Programs

American Indian Reference Book For Children And Young Adults,
collected by Barbara J. Kuipers (Libraries Unlimited, Portsmouth, NH, 1995);
ISBN: 1-56308-258-6; ISBN-13: 978-1-56308-258-0

The Best Years Of Their Lives, by Stephanie Zvirin
(American Library Association, Chicago, Second Edition, 1996);
ISBN-13: 978-0-8389-0686-6; ISBN-10: 0-8389-0686-9

A bibliography of books of interest to teenagers, dealing with crises and problems.

Black Authors and Illustrators of Children's Books, 3rd Edition,
by Barbara Rollock (Garland, New York, 1999);
ISBN-10: 0815320043;ISBN-13:978-0815320043

A biographical dictionary and bibliography.

---

*C.A.R.T.S. Culture Catalog: Multimedia Resources in Folklore, History,
Culture and the Arts,* (City Lore, New York, 2003; 212-529-1955;
http://www.citylore.org/online-store/scstore/)

Multicultural books for classroom use, dealing with all aspects of the curriculum.

Crossing Borders with Literature of Diversity, by Julia Candace Corliss,
Christopher-Gordon Publishers, Inc., Norwood MA, 1999; 800/934-8322;
http://www.christopher-gordon.com; ISBN 0-926842-81-1

Easy Reading: Book Series and Periodicals for Less Able Readers, 2nd Edition,
by Randall J. Ryder, Bonnie B. Graves and Michael F. Graves
(International Reading Association, Newark, DE, 1989); ISBN: 0872072347

For Adults Only: Reading Materials For Adult Literacy Students,
by F. E. Kazemak and P. Riggs, JOURNAL OF READING, v28, p726-31, May 1985

A Guide To Juvenile Books About Hispanic Peoples And Cultures,
by Isabel Scion (Scarecrow Press, Metuchen, NJ 08840) ISBN-0-8108-2462-0

Human and Anti-Human Values in Children's Books (Council on Interracial Books
for Children, 1841 Broadway, New York, NY 10023, 1976)

This book is out of print, but it may be available in libraries or in used book stores.

*Our Family, Our Friends and Our World: An Annotated Guide to Significant
Multicultural Books for Children and Teenagers,* by Lyn Miller-Lachmann
(Reed Reference Pub., New Providence, NJ, 1992) ISBN-0-8352-3025-2

Published by the New York Public Library, Fifth Ave. at 42nd St., New York,
http//www.nypl.org/

The Black Experience in Children's Books 2004 - An annotated list of recommended
books on the black experience for children ages 2-12, selected by a committee of
the New York Public Library's children's librarians. Sections include picture books,
stories, folklore, history, celebrations and reference.
2005, 64 pages, paperback, $8.00, ISBN 0-87104-768-3

Published by the New York Public Library, Fifth Ave. at 42nd St., New York,
http//www.nypl.org/

Books for the Teen Age 2006
A list of approximately 1,000 books arranged by
subject for teenagers and compiled annually by Young Adult librarians in the
Branch Libraries. 2006, 40 pages, paperback, $10.00, ISBN 0-87104-771-3

Published by the New York Public Library, Fifth Ave. at 42nd St., New York,
http//www.nypl.org/

Celebrating The Dream, 2001
A booklist compiled for teenage readers on the black experience; subjects include fiction, the arts, poetry, sports, and politics.
2001, 35 pages, paperback, $10.00, ISBN 0-87104-753-5

Published by the New York Public Library, Fifth Ave. at 42nd St., New York, http//www.nypl.org/

Children's Books 2005: One Hundred Titles For Reading And Sharing
One hundred titles published in 2005, selected as the best picture books, stories, and nonfiction for children from preschoolers to age 12.
2005, 16 pages, paperback, $3.00, ISBN 0-87104-770-5

Published by the New York Public Library, Fifth Ave. at 42nd St., New York, http//www.nypl.org/

Multicultural Publishers Exchange Catalog of Books By and About People of Color,
(Highsmith Co., Inc., W5527 Highway 106, P.O. Box 800, Fort Atkinson, WI 53538; 800-558-2110)

Paperback Books for Children: A Selected List Through Age Thirteen,
(Bank Street College, http//www.bnkst.edu/, New York, 1988)

"Resources to Identify Children's Books," Arlene M. Pillar, in *Invitation To Read,* ed. Bernice E. Cullinan (International Reading Association, Newark, DE, 1992) ISBN-0-87207-371-8

Publishers and Manufacturers of Games, Software, Video (VHS and DVD) Useful in Reading Programs

Home-made games are inexpensive, fun to make and use and very helpful in instruction. Many commercial games can easily be adapted for instructional use. The following are only a few of the manufacturers of games that you may find useful. In addition to the following, many book publishers also produce games:

Cardinal Industries, 21-01 51st Avenue, Long Island City, NY 11101; 718-784-3000; http://www.cardinalgames.com/contact.htm

Basic games, such as chess, checkers, bingo, dominoes and board games.

Childcraft, Educational Division, 2920 Old Tree Drive, Lancaster, PA 17603; 800-631-5652; https://www.childcrafteducation.com/

Constructive Playthings, 13201 Arrington Rd., Grandview, MO 64030; 800-448-7830; http://www.constplay.com/family/default.htm

Discovery Toys, DiscoveryChannelStore.com); 800-341-8697; http://www.discoverytoysinc.com/

Educational Activities, P.O. Box 87, Baldwin, NY 11510; 800-797-3223; http://www.edact.com/

Videos, software, multimedia, early childhood through adult.

Milton Bradley Company, Hasbro Inc., Pawtucket, RI, 888-836-7025; http://www.hasbro.com/miltonbradley

Board games and video games.

Parker Brothers, Hasbro Inc., Pawtucket, RI, 888-836-7025; http://www.hasbro.com/default.cfm?page=browse&brand=681

Pressman Toy Co., 121New England Avenue, Piscataway, NJ; 800/800-0298; http://www.pressmantoy.com/

Wordsearch and Wheel of Fortune

Instructional Computer Software and Games

An excellent resource for the use of the web is *1001 Best Websites For Educators*, by Timothy Hopkins, MS (Teacher Created Resources, Inc., Westminster, CA, http://www.teachercreated.com/); ISBN-0-7439-3877-1.

This book lists and describes more than 1,000 websites in 22 categories including Art, Child Development, Classroom and Behavior Management, Diversity, Geography/Environment, History/Social Studies, Language Arts, Reading First and Science. It is an invaluable resource for teachers who are comfortable using the computer.

Producers of software often permit purchasers to try their programs, usually for thirty days, if purchased on the internet. If purchasers do not find it useful, they are permitted to return it for a refund of the purchase price. Programs purchased over the counter do not have this privilege.

If your students are ready to do internet research in preparation for writing reports, you may refer them to Google (http://www.google.com/) or Yahoo (http://www.yahoo.com/), where they will find information on many subjects. Other helpful sites are http://www.infoplease.com/, http://www.bartleby.com/, http://www.howstuffworks.com, and http://www.wikipedia.com/, all of which will refer the student to a variety of almanacs, a dictionary, an atlas and encyclopedias.

Although computer software is often costly, there are several sources for inexpensive software. Some companies list instructional materials and games for a few dollars per disk; the programs on these disks are either in the public domain (which means that they are not copyrighted and may be used by anyone) or are "shareware." Authors of shareware permit purchasers to try their programs; if they like them and wish to take full advantage of them, users are requested to register with the author and pay a modest fee in addition to the initial purchase price. This is a convenient way to try programs that may be useful and enjoyable.

Compass Learning, Inc. 203 Colorado Street, Austin, TX 78701; 800/232-9556; (www.compasslearning.com)

Educational software in mathematics, science, English, reading.

Educational Activities Inc., 1937 Grand Ave., PO Box 87, Baldwin, NY 11510; 800/797-3223; www.edact.com

Videos, software, multimedia, early childhood through adult.

The M & M Software Library, (www.mm-soft.com)

Microsoft Corp., One Microsoft Way, Redmond, CA 98052; 800-642-7676; http://www.microsoft.com/

Milton Bradley Company, Hasbro Inc., Pawtucket, RI, 888-836-7025; http://www.hasbro.com/miltonbradley/

National Geographic Society, 1145 17th St., N.W., Washington, DC 20036; 888/225-5647; http://www.nationalgeographic.com/

One More Story, 54 White Street, 5th floor, New York, NY 10013; 212-925-9416; http://www.onemorestory.com/

On-loan library of the best of children's literature; child selects a book, sees it and hears it read to him.

Riverdeep, 100 Pine Street (Suite 1900), San Francisco, CA 94111; 415.659.2000 http://www.riverdeep.net/

This company now encompasses:
Broderbund Software, (http://www.broderbund.com/)
Edmark Corporation (http://www.riverdeep.net/)
The Learning Company (http://www.learningcompany.com/)
    Educational software

Tom Snyder Productions (Scholastic), 100 Talcott Avenue, Watertown, MA, 02472; 800-342-0236; http://www.tomsnyder.com/

Weston Woods/Scholastic (soon to be renamed Scholastic Classics), 730 Broadway, New York, NY 10003; 800-392-2179; http://teacher.scholastic.com/products/westonwoods/

Outstanding videos and DVD's of classic children's literature, encouraging reading. Excellent catalogue.

Periodicals of Interest to Your Students

For All Ages:

Black Enterprise: http://www.blackenterprise.com/

Consumer Reports: http://www.consumerreports.org/cro/index.htm

EbonyJet: http://www.ebonyjet.com/

Essence: http://www.essence.com/essence/

Family Circle: http://www.familycircle.com/

Hispanic Magazine: http://www.hispaniconline.com/magazine/

Ms: http://www.msmagazine.com/

National Geographic : http://www.nationalgeographic.com/ngm/0702/index.html

Natural History (from the American Museum of Natural History, New York): http://www.naturalhistorymag.com/

Newsweek: http://www.msnbc.msn.com/id/3032542/site/newsweek/

Parents: http://www.parents.com/

Popular Science: http://www.popsci.com/popsci/

Popular Mechanics: http://www.popularmechanics.com/

Reader's Digest: http://www.rd.com/

Time: http://www.time.com/time/

Upscale: http://www.upscalemagazine.com/portal/

For Grade School Children:

Cricket (Carus Publishing Corp.): http://www.cricketmag.com/home.asp
  Also *Babybug, Click, Ladybug, Spider*—for grade school children

Dolphin Log (The Cousteau Society): http://www.dolphinlog.org/frm_dolphinLog.html

Highlights for Children: http://www.highlights.com/

National Geographic Pathfinder Edition, and *Explorer Edition*
http://magma.nationalgeographic.com/ngexplorer/0209/teachers/faqs.html

Subscriptions Designed for Teachers in the Classroom:

News for You (New Readers Press) http://www.news-for-you.com/index_h.html

Ranger Rick (National Wildlife Federation)
http://www.nwf.org/kids/kzPage.cfm?siteid=3

Sports Illustrated for Kids
http://www.sikids.com/about_us/subscribe/index.html,
http://sikids.com/ SIKIDS.com is the online counterpart to Sports Illustrated For Kids
magazine

U*S* Kids (Children's Better Health Institute) http://www.cbhi.org/

Also: *Turtle, Humpty Dumpty, Playmate, Jack and Jill, Child's Life,* and *Children's Digest*

Weekly Reader, weekly newspaper in levels Pre-K to 12

The following five publications are produced by:

The Weekly Reader Corp., 3001 Cindel Drive,
Delran, NJ 08075800/446-3355
http://www.weeklyreader.com/

Know Your World Extra
Reading level 6 and up, 12 issues

Current Science
Grade Levels 6–12, 16 issues

Read Magazine
Grade levels 6–10, 16+ issues

Current Events
Grades 6–10, 25 issues

Weekly Reader
Pre K–K, 28 issues
1–2, 32 issues
3–6, 28 issues

Background Reading for the Instructor

Some of the books listed are out of print, and no longer available from the publishers. They are often available in used book stores, and can be searched for and purchased online by calling up such search companies as http://www.Abebooks.com/. They assist in locating bookstores that have the title you need; you then order directly from the bookstore, and receive the book in the mail.

All Spelled Out, by Betsy Rubin (Contemporary Books, Inc., Chicago)

The Art Of Teaching Writing, by Lucy McCormick Calkins (Heinemann)

Becoming Literate, by Marie M. Clay (Heinemann) ISBN-10: 0435085743; ISBN-13: 978-0435085742

Choosing Books for Children: A Commonsense Guide, by Betsy Hearne (Dell, New York) ISBN-10: 0252069285; ISBN-13: 978-0252069284

The Complete Theory to Practice Handbook of Adult Literacy: Curriculum Design and Teaching Approach, by Rena Soifer, et al.(Teachers College Press, New York)

Coping with Kids and School, by Linda Albert (E. P. Dutton, New York) ISBN-10:0345321758; ISBN-13:978-0345321756

Fact and Fiction: Literature Across the Curriculum, by Bernice E. Cullinan (International ReadingAssociation, Newark, DE)

Illiteracy, A National Dilemma, by D. Harman (Cambridge Adult Book Company, New York)

Literature Circle Resource Guide: Teaching Suggestions, Forms, Sample Book Lists and Databases, by Bonnie Campbell Hill, Katherine L. Schlick Noe, Nancy J. Johnson (Christopher-Gordon)

Mosaic of Thought, by Ellen Olive Keene and Susan Zimmerman (Heinemann)

The Multiple Intelligences of Reading and Writing, by Thomas Armstrong (Association for Supervision & Curriculum Development (ASCD) ISBN-10:0871207184; ISBN-13:978-0871207180, http://www.ascd.org/portal/site/ascd

The Read-Aloud Handbook, by Jim Trelease (Penguin Books, New York)

Solving Language Difficulties, by Nina Traub and Frances Bloom (Cambridge, Educators' Publishing Service)

Special Needs, Special Answers, by L. Pope, D. Edel and A. Haklay (Book-Lab, Inc.)
www.ezra-jack-keats.org

Tutor, by Lillie Pope (Book-Lab, Inc.) www.ezra-jack-keats.org

Why Didn't I Learn This In College? by Paula Rutherford (Just Ask Publications,
division of Attitudes, Skills and Knowledge) ISBN-10: 0966333616;
ISBN-13: 978-0966333619, http://askeducation.com/publications.htm

Of Special Interest to Those Who Teach English as a Second Language

Bringing Literacy to Life Issues and Options in Adult ESL Literacy, by H.S. Wrigley and
G.J.A. Guth (Laguirre International, San Mateo, CA)
ISBN: 0963370200 9780963370204

*Caring and Sharing in the Foreign Language Class: A Sourcebook on Humanistic
Techniques,* by G. Moskowitz (Newbury House, Cambridge, MA)
ISBN: 0-88377-098-9/0883770989

The Natural Approach, by S.D. Krashen and T.D. Terrell (Pergamon)
ISBN-10: 0080286518; ISBN-13:978-0080286518

Whole Language for Second Language Learners, by Y.S. Freeman and D.E. Freeman
(Heinemann, Portsmouth, NH) ISBN: 0435087231

Word Play, A Dictionary of Idioms, by Lillie Pope, Book Lab., Inc.,
www.ezra-jack-keats.org

Periodicals of Interest to the Instructor

Instructor, Scholastic Inc., 800/724-6527, http://www.scholastic.com/

Scholastic, Scholastic, Inc., 800/724-6527, http://www.scholastic.com/

Teacher, Editorial Projects in Education, 800/346-1834

Teaching Pre-K-8, http://www.neodata.com/teac/inquiry.shtml

Young Children, National Association for the Education of Young Children, (NAEYC)
P.O.Box 96270, Washington, D.C. 20090-6270, 800/424-2460, http://www.naeyc.org

Special Interest Associations and their Publications

American Association for Adult and Continuing Education (AAACE),
10111 Martin Luther King, Jr. Highway, Suite 200C, Bowie, MD 20720,
http://www.aaace.org
Adult Learning

American Library Association, 50 East Huron Street, Chicago, IL 60611,
800/545-2433, http://www.ala.oeg

Children with Attention Deficit Disorders (CHADD)
8181 Professional Place, Suite 150, Landover, MD 20785, 301/306-7070,
http://www.chadd.org/AM
The C.H.A.D.D.er Box

Council for Exceptional Children (CEC)
1110 North Glebe Road, Suite 300, Arlington, VA 22201, 888/232-7733,
http://www.cec.sped.org

International Dyslexia Association
Chester Bldg. (Suite 832), 8600 LaSalle Rd., Baltimore, MD 21286-2044,
800/222-3123, http://www.interdys.org
Perspectives

International Reading Association (IRA)
800 Barksdale Rd. (P.O. Box 8139), Newark, DE 19714, http://www.reading.org
*Reading Teacher, Journal Of Adolescent And Adult Literacy,
Reading Research Quarterly*

Laubach Literacy
1320 Jamesville Avenue (Box 131), Syracuse, NY 13210
315/422-9121, 888/528-2224, http://www.laubach.org

Learning Disabilities Association (LDA)
4156 Library Rd., Pittsburgh, PA 15234, http://www.ldanatl.org
LDA Newsbriefs

Literacy Assistance Center, Inc.
32 Broadway, 10th floor, New York, NY 10004, http://www.lacnyc.org
212/803-3300
Literacy Update

Literacy Partners, Inc.
  30 East 33rd Street, 6th floor, New York, NY 10016, 212/725-9200,
  http://www.literacypartners.org

Literacy Volunteers of America
  ProLiteracy Worldwide, 1320 Jamesville Avenue,
  Syracuse, NY 13210, 888/528-2224, Option 6, http://www.literacyvolunteers.org

National Council of Teachers of English (NCTE)
  1111 Kenyon Rd., Urbana, IL 61801, 877/369-6283, http://www.ncte.org

National Education Association (NEA)
  1201 16 Street, NW, Washington, DC 20036-3290, 202/833-4000, http://www.nea.org

Reading Is Fundamental, Inc. (RIF)
  1825 Connecticut Ave. NW (Suite 400), Washington, DC 20009,
  877-743-7323, http://www.rif.org

Teachers of English for Speakers of Other Languages (TESOL)
  700 So. Washington St. (Suite 200), Alexandria, VA 22314,
  888/547-3369, http://www.tesol.org
  TESOL Matters and Adult Education Newsletter

United Federation of Teachers (UFT)
  52 Broadway, New York, NY 10004 212/777-7500, http://www.uft.org

Appendix

What to Do About
Common Reading
Errors and Difficulties

Frequently Asked Questions

Helpful Resources

Glossary

Glossary

accent: the stress given to a syllable so that it will be more prominent than other syllables; a characteristic pronunciation influenced by the speaker's native language or regional background.

accountable talk: students meet in a small group to discuss their reading.

affix: prefix or suffix.

antonyms: words having opposite meanings, such as *up* and *down*.

articulation: (in speech) the formation of speech sounds; the quality of clarity of speech sounds.

attention span: the length of time an individual can concentrate without being distracted or losing interest.

auditory discrimination: the ability to hear and perceive differences between sounds that are similar but not the same, such as *p* and *b*. Also called **auditory perception.**

audiometer: instrument used to test hearing.

basal readers: graded series of readers traditionally used in reading instruction; vocabulary and sentence length and structure become more complex as the grade levels advance.

basic education: a course of study in which the basic tools of reading, arithmetic and writing are acquired; frequently applied to adult education classes.

big books: books printed with large type on pages as large as 18 by 24 inches; they are used when the teacher reads to the group, so that each student may see the pages at a distance.

blend: combine two sounds smoothly to produce a sound in which both are heard distinctly; a word formed by the fusion of two or more sounds.

classics: works of literature that are widely appreciated and expected to be appreciated for years to come, such as *Alice in Wonderland*, by Lewis Carroll.

coaching: one-to-one mentoring.

compound word: word that is made up of two or more words, such as *baseball* and *firefly*.

concept: idea. Concept may explain how a specific thing is classified, as the concept of color relates to red, green and blue; it may deal with an abstract thought like honesty or loyalty.

configuration clue: the general shape of a word, which helps the reader recognize the word.

consonant: letter that represents a speech sound produced by closing or narrowing the mouth (such as *b*, *m* and *s*) or the throat (such as *k*, *q* and *x*).

consonant equivalents: the two or three possible sounds of the consonants *s*, *c* and *g*.

Teach Anyone To Read: The No-Nonsense Guide

consonant blend: combination of the sounds of two or three consonants in which each sound is heard distinctly, such as *str* in *street*.

consonant digraph: combine two sounds smoothly to produce a sound in which both are heard distinctly; a word formed by the fusion of two or more sounds.

context clues: meaning of known words in a sentence or paragraph to reveal the pronunciation and meaning of an unfamiliar word.

cursive writing: style of writing in which the letters are connected; usually called handwriting.

decoding approach: an approach to reading instruction that emphasizes sounding out the written message. Phonics and linguistic methods are both decoding approaches.

derivative: word composed of a root word plus a prefix or suffix.

developmental reading instruction: reading instruction designed to teach the reading skills systematically. The term is usually applied to instruction for the beginning learner, as opposed to remedial reading instruction, which is for students who have failed to learn in a developmental reading program.

diagnostic checklist: a list of skills involved in the process of reading, in which the student's skills and weaknesses are recorded.

diagnostic test: a test designed for evaluating individual strengths and weaknesses in reading.

dialect: a variation of a language in which the words, usage and pronunciation are characteristic of a specific locality.

diphthong: combination of two vowel sounds that blend to become one, such as *oi, oy, ou, ow* and *ew.* Also called a **vowel blend.**

directional confusion: the inability of the reader to move the eye consistently from left to right; this results in reversals, such as *was* for *saw.*

disabled reader: a reader whose level of reading competence is significantly lower than is expected of him.

dyslexia: medical term that encompasses a variety of reading disabilities.

emergent reader: a term used to describe a "developing" reader of any age, beginning with infancy. The term is sometimes used to indicate that an individual has reached the level of "reading readiness."

ESL: (abbreviation) English as a Second Language.

experience chart: a printed or handwritten chart recording the details of an experience chosen by the student in the student's own words. This tool is equally useful in classroom and individual instruction. Sometimes called the **experience method.**

expected grade placement: the grade in which students of the same chronological age are usually grouped. For example, expected grade placement for a six-year-old is the first grade; for a fourteen-year-old, it is the ninth grade.

eye-span: the amount of written material that can be perceived by the eye in one fixation.

figurative language: words and phrases that contain figures of speech, such as idioms and metaphors, that are not meant to be interpreted literally.

flash cards: cards on which letters, words or phrases are written or printed; they are used for rapid drill in reading and arithmetic instruction.

frustration reading level: the level at which an individual's reading skills are inadequate. The reader loses fluency, makes five or more errors in 100 words and becomes tense and uncomfortable.

functional illiterate: a person who reads below the fifth-grade level.

guided reading: students and teacher read together in small groups.

holistic: a philosophy of education that considers the total individual, his temperament, learning style, interests, skills and deficits in order to facilitate learning.

homographs: words that are spelled the same but have different pronunciations and meanings, such as *sewer* (for waste disposal) and *sewer* (one who sews).

homonyms: words that sounds the same but have different meanings and sometimes different spellings, such as *to, too* and *two.*

homophones: words that sound the same but have different spellings and meanings, as *night* and *knight.*

idiom: an expression with a meaning peculiar to the culture in which it is used.

independent reading level: the highest reading level at which one can read fluently and with a minimum of error without assistance.

individual instruction: instruction given by a teacher to one student; one-to-one tutoring.

individualized instruction: instruction of a student based on a careful assessment of his needs. Each student, whether taught individually or in a group, usually proceeds at his own pace.

Initial Teaching Alphabet (ITA): a 44-letter alphabet designed in England by Sir James Pitman to simplify the learning of reading. Unlike the standard English alphabet, each letter stands for only one sound, and upper- and lower-case letters have the same shapes.

instructional reading level: the highest reading level at which one can read fluently under teacher supervision.

invented spelling: spelling made up by the beginning reader, usually by sounding out the words.

kinesthetic instruction: instruction making use of the muscle sense and movement. In reading, the kinesthetic sense is involved when the student traces the outlines of letters and words. Also called the **kinesthetic method.**

lateral dominance: the preference for use of one side of the body over the other, as being right-handed.

leveled libraries: library books graded according to reading level by a classroom teacher.

linguistics: the science of language; a method of teaching reading that emphasizes a decoding, or sounding-out, approach.

look-say method: learning to recognize a word by its shape. Also call the **sight method**.

manuscript writing: a style of handwriting adapted from the printed letter; each letter is separately shaped, in contrast with cursive writing, in which the letters are joined.

metaphor: a figure of speech in which a word or phrase that usually denotes one thing is used to describe something else; for example, *"All the world's a stage."*

mini lesson: reading aloud, the instructor models a skill.

mirror method: a method that involves using a mirror in which the reader reads the printed matter; this method is sometimes used for readers who make an extraordinary number of reversals.

multi-sensory approach: an approach to teaching reading that makes use of all of the senses: visual, auditory, phonic analysis, smell, taste, tactile and kinesthetic (sense of movement): tracing letters and words; raised letters, letters on sandpaper.

phoneme: a small unit of speech sound, as *m* in *mat*.

phonetics: the science of speech sounds; the system of sounds of a particular language.

phonics: the study of the sounds that letters represent; a technique of reading instruction that associates letters with their sounds, also known as the **phonic method.**

phonogram: a letter or group of letters representing a speech sound.

picture clue: a picture illustrating written matter that provides a clue to word recognition and meaning.

prefix: a syllable added to the beginning of a word to modify its meaning.

readability: a measure of the reading difficulty of a text, based on the length of words and sentences and the type of vocabulary.

read aloud: instructor reads to the group, usually at a level above the students' ability to read independently.

reading diagnosis: analysis of a student's reading competence and the exact nature of his skills and deficits. Reading diagnosis also attempts to determine the cause of the reading disability and to suggest remedial treatment.

reading level: the level of a reader's skills, expressed in terms of the school grade in which those skills are expected to have been mastered.

reading readiness: the level of developmental maturity the child must reach before formal reading instruction is expected to be effective. At this level, he is able to perceive similarities and differences in shapes, knows some of the letters and probably already recognizes several words at sight.

remedial reading instruction: see **developmental reading instruction.**

retarded reader: see **disabled reader.**

rigorous design: a plan to achieve standards.

root word: the base word, from which words are developed by the addition of prefixes and suffixes, such as *re work, work able.*

shared reading: the teacher reads to the group at a level usually too difficult for students to read independently, and shares her thoughts.

sight word: a word recognized automatically, usually by its shape.

sight method: teaching reading by having the reader respond to whole words rather than the sounds of the letters. Also called the **whole word method** and **sight word approach.**

structural analysis: analysis of a word by breaking it down to its parts: root, suffix, prefix; if it is a compound word, breaking it down to its component words.

scanning: rapid reading to gain an overall impression, or to find specific information, overlooking details. Also called **skimming**.

suffix: a letter or syllable added at the end of a word to modify its meaning.

syllable: a letter or group of letters representing a vowel sound; it may or may not contain one or more consonants.

syllabication: the process of dividing a word into single syllables.

synonyms: words that have similar meanings but are spelled and pronounced differently, such as *large* and *big*.

tachistoscope: a device that exposes material for a brief period of time so that it must be read at a glance.

TESOL: (acronym) Teaching (Teachers) of English to Speakers of Other Languages.

tool subject: a subject involving the learning of a skill that is necessary for the learning of other subjects: reading, writing, arithmetic.

trade book: a book published for sale through bookstores and booksellers.

visual discrimination: the ability to distinguish likenesses and differences between shapes, particularly letters and words. Also called **visual perception.**

vowel: a letter representing a sound made with the mouth open. The vowel letters are *a, e, i, o, u.* Sometimes *y* is used as a vowel.

vowel digraph: a combination of two vowels, or a vowel followed by *w,* which represents a single speech sound: *ai, ea, ie, oa, ay, ea, oo, au, ei, ow, aw.* Also called a **vowel team.**

whole language: a holistic approach to the teaching of reading, in which the reading, writing, listening and speaking are integrated.

whole word method: see **sight method.**

word: a symbol of an idea; the smallest unit representing an idea.

word attack skills: word analysis.

word-by-word reading: reading at a halting pace, in which every word presents to the reader an obstacle that must be mastered before the next word is attacked.

word discrimination: the ability to distinguish one word from another.

word families: groups of rhyming words containing identical word elements, used in teaching word recognition. The student is drilled in recognizing the variable elements in word families such as *bat, hat, fat, cat, rat.*

word wheel: a device used to practice in word attack skills, consisting of two circular cards printed with different word elements clipped together.

workbook: practice book, in which the student writes, that provides practice in reading skills. Workbooks may accompany the textbook or may be used independently.

To obtain additional copies of this book contact us at:
foundation@ezra-jack-keats.org or call 718/965-1266

NOTES

NOTES